SERENITY THROUGH GOD 1

NICOLE

authorHOUSE®

AuthorHouse™
1663 Liberty Drive
Bloomington, IN 47403
www.authorhouse.com
Phone: 1 (800) 839-8640

Published by AuthorHouse 02/06/2017

ISBN: 978-1-5049-7756-2 (sc)
ISBN: 978-1-5049-7755-5 (e)

Library of Congress Control Number: 2017901431

Print information available on the last page.

*Any people depicted in stock imagery provided by Thinkstock are
models, and such images are being used for illustrative purposes only.
Certain stock imagery © Thinkstock.*

This book is printed on acid-free paper.

*Because of the dynamic nature of the Internet, any web
addresses or links contained in this book may have changed
since publication and may no longer be valid. The views
expressed in this work are solely those of the author and do
not necessarily reflect the views of the publisher, and the
publisher hereby disclaims any responsibility for them.*

CONTENTS

CHAPTER 1

ↀↀ

I had lived in Colorado all my life,
so when my mom and dad said
were moving,
all I could think about
is all my friends,
I'd be losing.
We packed the stuff we needed,
in our car,
I wanted to stay here in Colorado,
"daddy please can we just go back?"
"No we have come too far." He said
My mother and father felt,
our dad being a trucker,
was the best thing to do,
"when daddy is in town,
He'll be able to see you." Said mom
We finally reached Springfield Illinois,
and visited our family,
like aunt,
for she always had open arms,
of love;
For my brothers and me.
My parents found a house,
for us to live in,
my mother found a job,
and even a babysitter,
Who was next of kin.
When Monday rolled around,
back to the babysitter,

he would play strange games,
with my siblings and I;
He was a real kidder.
Oh how I loved my father and mother,
so when us kids heard them arguing,
and fighting,
We would all cuddle together.
We didn't understand,
how somebody who say's,
"they love you"
could come home,
after weeks on the road;
Just to abuse you.
My father told my older sibling,
"If you don't quit soiling in your diaper,
You're going to get a whipping."
My brother didn't make it,
to the bathroom in time,
so my father removed it,
and rubbed it in his face;
Leaving him crying.
My mother had nobody,
to turn to,
to escape from the abuse,
she would cry as she said to us,
"I don't know what to do."
My mother never told us,
what her and dad fought about,
daddy came home drunk,

4

taking mom into their bedroom;
And begin to shout.
When daddy didn't go to the bars,
and drink,
he would come home,
hugging us all,
For he took time to think.
Every work day,
feeling of fear was in my heart,
for these strange games,
my relative made us play,
Was getting ready to start.
He told my siblings and I,
"this is what were going to do
I'm taking your sister,
in the bedroom with me,
And this is what you will do.
You boys will hang,
from these door ledges,
if you interrupt me,
because of falling,
I will be very angry,
and you may just push me;
Over the edge."
I was taken into his bedroom,
and he tells me,
warning us, "If tell you about this,
I'll kill you; just wait and see."
He would pick me up,

and throw me onto his bed,
taking my clothes off,
for I have nothing left to shed
then off came his clothes,
yelling at me;
He laid there comfortably,

urinating my mouth,
yelling at me;
"Swallow it you little wh-re."
My cousin would hear,
a kid drop to the floor,
the cousin say's, "fine you like pain
I'll give you some more."
The cousin laid flat on his back,
his legs spread apart,
he tells my brother,
"stand between my legs."
then bangs them together,
inflicting pain while having to watch,
Just broke my heart.
My cousin did this every weekday,
for three years,
because he felt the thrill of power,
from doing it,
while my two brothers,
And I shed tears.

The Monster

You have this adult relative,
who baby-sits you every day,
hanging you and your siblings,
on door frames,
He tells you "if you fall you will pay."
Your fingers are getting sore,
and turning red,
he yell's "swallow it,"
one of the siblings,
would fall from the ledge,
I prayed he'll quit.
The cousin gets mad at your siblings,
for falling,
then makes the sibling,
stand between his legs,
the cousin bangs them together;
For interrupting his fun by calling.
He hangs your brother,
back on the door ledge,
tells the boy,
"if you fall again you'll make me mad
You may even push me over the edge."
My father's boss said,
"I'm moving the business to Colorado,
if you want to continue working for me,
That's where you'll have to go."
Once again everything is getting left behind,

except necessities, but I was still happy
for I was escaping from the monster;
Who was so unkind.
My parents traveled day and night,
only stopping to get gas, food and ice,
so we all had something to eat and drink,
Which was nice.
During the daytime,
when us kids could see,
we would play this paper game,
Called hangman; to keep us busy.
We had to watch our spending,
while traveling back to Colorado,
so my parents would have money,
to rent a house,
And not get stuck with nowhere to go.
My mother and father took turns,
sitting behind the wheel,
for my father had to be in Colorado,
the following week;
For that was the deal.
I was getting tired
I needed to go to sleep,
my father was driving,
so I asked him to wake me up,
when I can see the mountains,
When he did; all I felt was relief.
As soon as I could see,
we was in Colorado,

I knew,
We didn't have much farther to go.
My father and mother found a home,
for us to live in,
and us six kids,
Were able to go to the same school again.
A few days after arriving in Colorado,
my father's boss told him,
"I have a load for you to haul,
You'll have to leave tomorrow."
Once again,
my mother lies in her bed,
all alone,
wondering about,
how will she take care of us,
On her own.
Mom would get up,
and tuck us children into bed,
kisses her son's goodnight,
walks into my room,
sees me lying on the floor;
With blood on my head.
My mom screams,
"God why are you doing this to me?
because of having children out of wedlock,
Is that why your punishing me."
My brothers would come to my room,
And ask mom "what's wrong with sissy?"
"don't worry baby," She said

"She's just different; than you and me."
Mom would tell us kids to go outside,
and play for a while,
the six of us would play,
ring around the rosie,
when it came time to stand back up;
I would just sit in the dirt pile.
Your siblings yelling Mommy,
"what's wrong with Sue,"
my mother would run outside,
to see what was wrong;
But she didn't know what to do.
Mom never seen this action before,
so when I would have these episodes,
all she could do, is keep my head;
From hitting the floor.
God tell me,
what's wrong with my baby,
show me where to take her,
For mom didn't know I had Epilepsy.

Wild Child

A woman gives birth to a child,
that God had given her,
she sees it shake,
tremble and hyperventilate,
feeling helpless;
Because there's no cure.
A woman finds the child,
passed out on the floor,
saliva and blood leaking out her mouth,
Yelling "I can't take this anymore."
My mom figured fine,
I'll just keep my child inside,
and no others have to see,
these happenings;
As if there was something to hide.
She would get embarrassed,
or ashamed,
as if I had control over it,
But mom; had no one else to blame.
My siblings, would yell to mom,
"I don't know what to do,"
mom would say,
"don't worry baby;
She's just not like me and you."
The lady withdraws her love,
from her child,
feeling it's evil or cursed,

that's why she goes wild,
mom asking herself;
"What could be worse?"
I kneel down beside my bed,
asking God let my mom see,
I'm not an evil thing,
It's just all in her head.

We got re-enrolled in school,
and seen some of my old friends,
I didn't have many though,
for after they would see me seize;
Friendships just seem to end.
All the kids on the bus,
had a fear of me,
for they were afraid,
Of catching my disease; Epilepsy.
I always got called stupid names,
like seizure baby,
always getting told
"you'll never become anything"
In my mind saying we'll see.
I would go home,
after being called every cruel name,
asking mommy,
"Why do the other kids pick on me?"
mom told me;
"they don't look at you the same,
Because you have a disability."

I would go and have a good cry,
in my bedroom,
then mom would yell up the stairs,
"Dinners going to be done soon."
All six of us kids would sit,
at the dinner table with our mother,
but the only males who sat there,
Were my brothers.
My father worked for a trucking company,
he would be gone for days or weeks,
then came the bad time,
when his boss said, "I'm shutting down
It's too much for me."
Dad took a couple days off,
to spend with the family,
soon all the free time ended,
he had to find a way;
To support his family.
Dad searched day after day,
he knew mechanics from the military,
he was able to find work,
With a decent pay.
Dad worked for him,
down on eighth street,
he would come home from work,
Feeling all tired and beat.
Dad had to work late hours,
like his boss said,
if he wanted to continue,

to feed us;
And keep a roof over our head.
My mom and us kids,
didn't get to see dad a lot,
because his boss wanted,
all the cars fixed,
so he could put them up for sale;
On the lot.
My family didn't get to go to out,
and meet others,
my friends talked about,
how they went to amusement parks,
With their sister and brothers.
The last day I seen dad,
I was only seven,
he came home,
collapsed to the floor,
it was then;
That God took him to heaven.

CHAPTER 2

৵৶

Daddy Don't Leave Me

Daddy you've come home,
after a seven or eight day trip,
oh no daddy your falling,
And it's not from a slip.
Daddy come on,
your just lying there on the floor,
alright dad you can open your eyes,
This isn't funny anymore.
Dad why are you breathing so heavy,
And grabbing your chest?
oh I understand,
You just need some rest.
My dad is yelling at mom,
saying this hurts,
it's ok daddy,
they're coming to help you,
But the pain keeps getting worse.
He says to me,
it's ok baby I'll always love you,
no daddy no,
for if you leave this world,
How will we make it without you?
Daddy the paramedics are here,
you'll be ok,
but they get there too late,
for he never returned;
God had taken him away.

My mother told us to stay at home,
she would let us know,
how he's doing,
but when she came home;
She walked through the door alone.
My father may have died physically,
but I still remember,
running my fingers through his hair,
and nobody can take those memories;
From me.

After dad died,
from his massive coronary,
I seen less of mom,
but I needed a woman to talk to;
But mom wasn't there to teach me.
Mom was scared,
of being alone all her life,
so she started bar hopping,
to find a man who loved her enough,
To make her his wife.
My mom went from being,
a loving homemaker,
to a female who feared,
nobody would take care of her.
My mom had six kids to raise,
but needed,
somebody to love her,
and us kids;
And for one to hear a praise.
After spending many months,
down at the bar,
mom met this man,
who had no home of his own,
He didn't even have a car.
The man moved in right away,
he didn't have a job,
to help with bills,
yet mom let him stay,
hoping to be together;

Till their dying day.
That same year,
mom and this man,
made vows to each other,
but he showed no love,
To myself or my brothers.
When my mom and him would leave,
they were happy and excited to go out,
but when each of them got back;
Us kids would grieve.
All us kids knew the next day,
we would see bruises on her,
I asked why don't we just leave,
But mom was too insecure.
They kept going to the bars,
all the time,
He remained,
a cold hearted person,
my mom shied away,
I felt like her world;
Was separated from mine.
My stepdad and mom,
took us too,
seeing no reason
for getting drunk,
then people,
Did things; they normally wouldn't do.
My stepdad had friends,
who played instruments just like him,

so he asked them,
If they wanted to start playing again.
All six of them,
would play their instruments,
while I would sing,
going from bar to bar,
To see how much money; it would bring.
I would always have five dollars,
handed to me,
back then;
Five dollars was like a twenty.
It was quite the life,
playing and singing in the bars,
after a couple of years,
we became popular hearing people say;
Here they are.
Our band broke up after a while,
no longer playing or singing,
And making people smile.
We moved out to a little town,
called security,
I met a few people who liked me,
Even though I had a disability.
The town had a tower,
with black letters on it,
so if I would get lost,
I would know how to find it.
I prayed the alcohol,
would be too far away,

for my mom and stepped,
To go and get drunk and stray.
We met our neighbors across the street,
I knew their daughter from school,
the family always invited us over
They were so sweet.
They're daughter was my best friend,
for a long time,
we played hopscotch at school,
she knew I had seizures,
But she didn't mind.
We lived in security for quite a while,
yet other than having my special friend,
I had no reason to smile.
Every day after going home,
from school,
I'd see my stepdad tipsy or drunk,
Acting like a fool.
My parents made alcohol,
the most important thing in their life,
my stepdad always wanted to argue,
sometimes became violent;
Then beat up his wife.
My stepdad would come home drunk,
late at night,
he would wake me, telling me;
"Get up and do your chores right."
I would try to hurry,
because I had school the next day,

but when I went to school feeling drug out,
somebody reported it;
And took all six of us kids away.
Social services removed us six kids,
from our home,
told my mom and stepdad,
"you won't get your kids back;
Until you can leave the alcohol alone."
They separated us kids into two's,
my younger brother asked,
"How will we ever see mommy again?"
I said it's ok,
we'll run away, and find the house we lived in.
We figured out,
what area our house was in,
the next step was to escape,
Without nobody knowing.
I told my baby brother,
we'll find mommy,
we'll leave tomorrow, when nobody's around
you and me;
How hard can it possibly be.
The nursery we lived in,
was on cascade,
we
had to find a way to academy;
Then we knew, we would have it made.
We made it to Circle drive,
then hitch hiked, to academy,

hoping to get back alive.
This man stopped,
giving us a ride to academy,
after dropping us off,
we seen that tower;
That said security. We were about to see,
our mommy again,
we didn't know,
that man had called the police;
telling them where we had been.
The police contacted DHS,
telling our caseworker,
they must be heading home;
For they know nobody else out there.
"We walked pass our school,
till we came to cactus drive,
we were so wore out and tired,
we didn't think
We would make it alive.
We thought we would be safe and sound,
suddenly a policeman,
pulled up,
taking us go back to the nursery;
For we were found.
The caseworker,
took my brother and me,
to the nursery,
they put me into a group home;
To separate my brother and me.

I spent many months,
in a group home called chins-up,
I would get told over and over,
"maybe you'll go home next month,"
I was just ready to give up.
Then the system,
placed me in a foster home,
the foster parents,
never expressed care or love,
I felt so alone.
I returned to the foster home,
after school one day,
there stood the social worker,
she told me;
"You get to go home today."
The social worker had taken
all six of us kids back home,
I hugged mom,
as soon as I seen her,
Oh mom I felt so alone.
I asked mom,
"please don't drink again"
I haven't had anybody to talk to,
You don't know how lonely I've been.
We had to go to counseling,
week after week,
expressing feelings to each other,
Then the other would speak.
The counselor asking us kids,

"Well how can this problem be solved?"
but after the sessions,
my relationship with my siblings;
Just seemed to dissolve.
One of my brothers,
kept going out stealing,
not caring about Mom's tears
He didn't care how mom was feeling.
My stepdad said
"let's leave the state,
then we won't have to do,
what they say
Especially the stuff I hate."
My stepdad assured mom,
he could make a lot of money,
then we won't have to answer to anybody,
"Let's go honey."
He convinced mom
to go to New Orleans,
when we got there,
we were broke,
No money to buy even beans.
We ate at the soup kitchen,
they always served,
rice and beans,
I hoped God would hear;
what I was wishing
He promised he'd get a job,
but all he did was drink beer,

while mom worked,
He laid around; like a slob.
My mom got a job,
as a waitress,
she struggled to feed us,
He wouldn't help;
He could care less.
My stepdad met two friends,
It made me sick, I wanted to die.
I told my parents,
what I was asked to do,
my stepdad never confronted my friend,
that's not what a loving parent;
Would do.
I just wanted a warm bed,
a place to call home,
where at any time,
I could lay down my head.
My stepdad met a guy,
at the Mardi-Gra,
the guy told him
I need someone
to clean my house;
That's all.
My stepdad told the man,
sending a younger sibling and me
telling us, go do it I know you can.
He kept sending us over to this house,

The man made my brother
clean his house,
while he took me into his room,
exposing his body;
to me, what a louse.
After doing the cleaning,
he returned me to the car,
we lived in,
knowing I'd see him again next week,
to arouse him again.

I thought parents,
protected their children,
then why was I constantly sent,
to these perverts house, again;
and again.
God if you are really real,
where's the love and honor,
I should be allowed to feel.
After living like this,
week after week for a year,
I asked my mom,
after work one day,
"Can we leave New Orleans?
I can't stand the way people live here.
We have no place to call home,
always eating at the soup kitchen,
because we couldn't afford,
To buy food of our own.

Flying cockroaches,
everywhere you go,
missing out on school,
For two years in a row.
Dad just lied,
about getting a job,
all he does is take your tips,
buys alcohol;
And lays around like a slob."
Mom said,
"I don't like working,
at Pitt Grill either,
but I have to,
so we can buy a starter
for our car;
And leave here."
My mom told my stepdad
"no more,
you're going to get a job,
on a shrimp boat,
I just can't take it anymore."
My stepdads reply was,
"I can't without an I.D,
I'll have to go to Colorado,
And you'll have to wait for me."
Mom needed to sell the car,
while dad was gone,
but dads friend stole it,
He knew it was wrong.

My dad's friends started arguing,
with another man there,
one pulled out this mecheddi,
and killed the guy;
He didn't care.
A police officer,
owned the trailer park,
and the bar in front of it,
a witness called in the plate number,
It wasn't hard to trace it.
My mom told the officer,
"he stole my vehicle"
she told him he couldn't drive it,
Because it would be illegal,
having no car or a place to live
the police officers got together,
To see what they could give.
My stepdad sent my mom a letter,
saying he was sorry
"but he can't come back,
to get the kids and you.
Mom sold our color TV,
and fan,
to the trailer park owner, giving all he can.
A piece of paper and keys,
was handed to mom,
by the owners wife, saying; have a good life.
We packed what we still had,
and headed back to Colorado,

"Mom will this beaten up car make it," I asked
She said "I don't know."
Mom drove every day and night,
neglecting herself from any sleep,
I prayed let us make it back all right.
When I woke up,
I knew we were in Colorado,
but we didn't make it all the way,
the car broke down;
In Pueblo.
My mom called,
the only person she knew,
mom asked her,
"Can you pick up the kid's and
me? she said; where are
you?"

CHAPTER 3

❧

Mom's friend
let us stay at their home,
the next month,
We rented a home of our own.
We moved into a house,
in stratmoor valley,
school was getting ready to start,
I was anxious yet it was scary.
What if I have a seizure in school,
will they stare and laugh at me,
And think I'm a fool.
After going to school,
that first day,
going home to do homework,
Then watch T.V; day to day.
I was surprised
when I returned home,
I seen that mom was not alone.
My mom let my stepdad,
move back in,
she knew
he wasn't going to keep his promise,
To not drink again.
I laid on mom and dad's bed,
while watching a movie,
while mom made popcorn,
Suddenly something slid inside me.
I didn't watch,
the movie anymore,

I went
to my bedroom;
slamming the door.
The next day,
I tried to tell my mom,
what my stepdad did to me,
he denied it,
She believed him; not me.
While laying in bed, I felt myself dying inside,
I was going to lose my mom;
because of his pride.
I asked myself what did I do,
that was so wrong,
it's not like I led him on,
Yet he's at home; and I'm gone.
I didn't want to go to another foster home,
so I overdosed, for I had nobody;
I was alone.
I just felt the need,
to die every day,
so I kept overdosing,
Till the state took me away.
Social Services placed me,
in the state hospital,
some kids there liked cutting,
Others attempted to kill.
I quit believing in God,
and hated all men,
for if there was a God,

Why did all these things happen.
After thirty days,
the state released me,
to my mother,
I didn't want to live in fear;
So I told another.
I reported my stepdad,
to the school nurse,
she asked
"Did you tell your mother"?
I said yes; "I told her first."
A social worker and police officer,
came to the school,
other kids were staring at me,
I felt like a fool.
I was then taken to my home,
they let me grab clothes,
as I walked out of the house,
I felt so alone.
The social worker took me,
to a foster home in security,
It wasn't like the other foster home,
These ones cared about me cared about me.
I actually liked it there,
their daughter played jacks with me,
and do each other's hair

Their son wasn't a cold,
and heartless guy,

when he went places,
He sometimes invited; my foster sister and I.
I still call my foster mom
for God has taken my real Dad,
But she's still here thankfully, not gone.
The last time I visited my foster mom,
she didn't care anymore,
For her true love was now gone.

A Second Home

You opened your heart and your door,
to children who were abused,
Unloved and just not cared for.
You and dad took care of us,
let us into your home,
welcomed us with open arms;
As if we were your own.
Because of the abuse,
that was done to me,
I was leery of letting you or dad,
Get close to me.
From the nineteen seventy's,
to the current time,
we have kept in contact,
Making your life a part of mine.
When the Department of Human Services,
came and took me back,
my only fear was,
I would never again see you;
or be able to come back.

I still keep in contact,
with my foster mom,
I no longer live with her,
but the memories,
Will be never be gone.
Human Services

took me back home,
feeling only fear
knowing my stepdad;
Wouldn't leave me alone.
I felt stuck with nowhere to go,
I had no relatives to turn to,
All my relatives,
lived outside Colorado.
I asked the only friend,
"what can I do?"
she said,
"My friend's roommate likes you."
My friend introduced me,
to three people,
who lived there,
noticing the guy spoken about;
did care.

My virginity was gone,
I woke up the next day in fear,
spending time together one time,
may take away my future.
if my and John's stupidity,

If last night's fun,
Created a life, what do I do?
I can't be a mom,
I don't even know how;
To be a wife.

I felt obligated to marry John,
when he asked me to,
for I slept with him
Before I said; I Do.
I married at the age of fifteen,
I didn't know how to be a wife,
I just needed a place, to lay my head;
And stay clean.
Just a few weeks after saying I Do,
he received orders for Korea,
"Where will I live?"
he told said "My parents will care for you."
We traveled to Yukon Oklahoma,
to live with his family,
I'd never met them,
not knowing if they would
like me.
my husband told his parents,
about my epilepsy,
and asked them, to pick up my pills monthly.
"To pick up my pills for monthly.
His family didn't believe in pills

just receive the holy ghost,
the Lord will heal you; he will."
The ambulance constantly coming,
because of seizing, his mom kept saying
they would quit
If you started believing.

41

After living a few months that way,
I called and asked my mother,
to come and get me,
Otherwise I may never see another day.
My mother pull up in front of their home,
I grabbed my bags to walk out,
my husband's dad tried to stop me,
I told him "leave me alone."
After my mother and I got back to Colorado,
I moved into one of her apartments,
One they call a studio.
There was only a few months left,
before John would come home,
little did I know;
He wasn't spending his nights alone.
Military guy's constantly partying,
in the apartment yard,
passing pictures around,
one had my husband with another woman;
So divorcing him wasn't hard.
For if you truly had loved me,
and I truly loved you,
you wouldn't have cheated,
and divorcing you;
Would have been hard to do.

A Marriage of convenience

I met you,
through a friend of mine,
I had the chance to escape being raped,
all would disappear;
my life would be fine.
When I married you,
we were only friends in my eyes,
I knew nothing about relationships,
When we took our vows;
I repeated words of lies.
I am sorry I lied to you,
using the words I love you,
you made me live in Oklahoma,
while you were in Korea;
Was the worst thing you could do.
You never warned me,
about your family's religious beliefs,
that I can't take no pills,
All my body could feel is grief.
I called my mom,
asking her to come and get me,
I needed someone to come,
And set me free.
I moved back to Colorado,
and moved into one of my mom's efficiencies,
so when military guy's,
would pass around pictures,

You were in one of them; but not with me.
Don't let your head swell,
for I didn't hurt or mourn over you,
I took the picture downtown,
Filed for divorce; it was actually easy to do.

After I was divorced I felt so free,
I had nothing tying me down,
And now I could be me.
I called my girlfriend from high school,
thinking I'd never see her again,
when I seen her; it was so cool.
We went to the clubs all the time,
she liked the raiders inn,
that's where she hung out,
With the wild kind.
The NCO club,
is the one I wanted to go to,
for the men were more mature,
the club was more quiet;
And the men had more respect for you.
I never had the chance,
to have a dating life,
for the first guy I met,
I ended up becoming his wife.
she talked to a lot of guy's she knew,
asking her if that's,
how you get dates?"
saying Just do what I do.

She was forward,
when it came to guys,
It was hard for me,
I was very shy.
My girlfriend left the club with a guy,
I seen this man several times,
he came to me with a drink,
saying "you were crying why?"
"My girlfriend left the club,
without even telling me,
I don't have a way home
the man said I can take you home.
We introduced ourselves
while walking out the bar,
I told him I don't live close,
It's kind of far.
He said,
that he had seen me before too,
that's why I go to there,
you can hear;
what another is saying to you.
What another is saying to you.
We went to another place,
as our conversation continued,
I could tell he was interested in me,
By the look on his face.
I was worried,
about getting home safely,
he offered to take me,

I didn't know him;
It was scary.
My girlfriend
never showed back up,
so I asked him to take me home,
I couldn't believe my friend dumped me;
Leaving me alone.
After he had got me back
to my home,
he asked,
if I'd go out with him,
that he wouldn't leave me alone.
He handed me his phone number,
I decided to go out with him,
then dialed his number
he said; "will you go out with me"?
I said "sure."
Every weekend our date just got better,
he took me to fancy restaurants,
taking my jacket off,
I felt like a princess;
When we were together.
After a few months of dating you,
I seen everything I wanted in a man,
and he seemed to want the same goals;
In life too.
He had told me of his past,
I told him mine,
asking while looking at him,

is that suppose to change my mind.
I told him,
"I have more ghosts in my closet,
than you do"
"that don't matter;
If a man truly loves you."
All that matters,
is I love you and you love me,
and the future Nicole,
Is who I want you to be."
I sat there in total disbelief,
after all he knew about me,
he still loved me, for who I was;
What a relief.
My second husband got down on one knee,
and popped the question,
not knowing by saying yes that evening,
I'd learn a hard lesson.
The wedding wasn't like,
I wanted it to be,
my second husband told me,
when we have enough money saved,
we'll have a big wedding;
That was his promise to me.
After the wedding took place,
my life turned around,
sad to say it wasn't for the better,
Was it because; he no longer felt free?
And felt bound.

The night we said I do,
he yelled out what he hated about me,
then started beating me, asking myself;
what happened to I love you.
The first couple months,
he took me out with him all the time,
he was nice to me in public,
at home he was mean;
I felt like I was losing my mind.
I told him "I can't take this anymore,
either stop drinking,
or pack your stuff up,
And walk out that door."
He begged and pleaded,
"please don't leave me,
I want to be with you forever,
And have a family."
For a couple months,
I seen that man I had before,
he even went to bed with me,
I wasn't sleeping alone anymore.
I went to my obstetrician,
she told me your going to have a baby,
I didn't know whether to cry or be happy.
When I told him the news,
he was so happy,
he didn't care if it was a girl,
but said "If it's a boy;
He gets named after me."

I was proud of him,
for he quit drinking,
when he was sober,
he insisted on cooking,
this was too good to be true;
Is what I was thinking.
When we would go to bed at night,
he would rub my belly,
talking to it saying,
"It's O.K son, Everything will be all right."
After I was a few months pregnant,
the Dr did an ultrasound,
I told my husband it's a boy,
that moment was the time,
I seen his heart filled with joy.
I decided to do the cooking the next day,
so he could relax when he came home,
instead he took the dish I made,
And threw it away.
I felt hurt and so angry inside,
for the work I did,
trying to make him happy wasn't enough,
I just sat down and cried.
He started calling me names,
and accusing me of cheating,
he knocked me over the couch,
I had a fear of losing my baby;
Because of taking a beating.
he showed no remorse,

for the damage he had done,
he just went to sleep,
Not caring if I was all right; or his son.
I had a discussion with him the next day,
I told him, "You could have killed our baby,
I can't continue to live this way."
He told me,
"It wouldn't have happened,
if you would have stayed away from me,"
these are words spoken from a person;
Who says he loves me.
All I could do was sit and cry,
Asking God why me?
I've been a good wife to him,
It's not like I didn't try.
After he left for work that day,
I tried to find someone to turn to,
for if I wanted my baby to live;
I had to get away.

The Two-sided Man

We dated for so long,
you were just the kind of guy,
every woman would dream of being with,
My love for you was strong.
I thought you felt the same way,
you treated me like a princess,
showed so much affection;
Then it just ended one day.
The day people say I do,
should be the happiest day of their life,
knowing someone loves you,
Enough to make you his wife.
On our wedding day you got wasted,
then we got to the home,
that we were suppose to live our lives together,
and you told me everything about me;
That you hated.
The next day,
after seeing what damage you had done,
you would just say,
You see these bruises?
if you would stay away from me;
You wouldn't have none.
Then you quit taking me out with you,
so when you would come home,
you would ask,
Who have you been screwing?

then beat me;
Till I was black and blue.
After being married a few months,
I told you we were going to have a child,
you punched the hell out of me,
knocking me over the couch,
You just went wild.
The next week you disappeared into thin air,
went AWOL from the army,
You couldn't be found anywhere.

I couldn't ask my siblings to help me,
in their hearts,
were just feelings;
Of hatred and jealousy.

Reality Is Embarrassing

My brother who is older than I,
Quits having contact with me,
because I tell him I can't go somewhere with him;
he says that's a damn lie.
I told you no because of my medical disability,
for I have limitations, but you can't face reality.

My oldest brother calls,
and asks if he can see me,
I tell him yeah that would be nice,
he walks in the gaming place;
a drunk is all I see.

You already know
I'm living what could be my last day,
I show my feelings about our life,
through my poetry,
you tell me you don't want to read it;
just get it away.
I ask you what's wrong with my poetry?
Nothing I just can't deal with it right now,
here we go again the fear of reality.

My brother who is one year younger,
hasn't had anything to do with me for years,
for I'm not rich enough for him, for
his love for money; is a stronger hunger.
I am not normal to you, because I take pills,

In your eyes epilepsy isn't normal,
so what will you do if your child collapses;
and suddenly becomes ill.
Will the love for your child, suddenly disappear?
Like it did towards me,
or will you be able to overcome that fear;
and face reality.

My younger brother
has never had the desire to be close to me.
all he feels is anger towards my mom and me,
thinking she favored me;
for all he feels is jealousy.
He called me a couple weeks ago,
saying, "if I didn't hear you almost died,
I still wouldn't be calling you now"
I just thought I'd let you know.
He said all I want to know is if you're a Christian,
I said yes I became one years ago,
he read the poem I wrote for him,
after reading it; anger struck again.
For he denies all he's done wrong,
once again, another sibling living in denial,
for you will have a sad life,
until you admit to yourselves;
that you have lived in sin all along.
It may have taken our mom a few lessons,
to open her eyes,
for she no longer takes time for granted,
and spends quality time with my kids and I.

I just wanted a family
that all people dream of,
siblings that stood by you,
no matter what;
to have that house full of love.
My past two husbands
had either abandoned or cheated on me,
I kept asking myself,
in the name of God;
what's wrong with me.
I put my heart and soul,
into believing these guys,
then they both enforced actions,
they said they didn't believe in;
for their words were just lies.
Because of these two men,
I had been married to,
I promised myself,
to never trust another,
no matter what they would say or do.
I felt so much hatred,
and didn't trust anybody,
for all the ones I opened up to,
ended up leaving me.
I would study my face,
when I looked into the mirror,
asking God what's wrong with me?
What were these guys saying;

that I couldn't hear. I didn't know
what I was going to do,
for now I was pregnant,
no job; with nobody to turn to.
I didn't know how to care for a baby,
or what my feelings for it would be,
because of the abuse,
it's dad had done to me.
I asked my mother what do I do,
after this month is over,
I have no place to live,
she offered her extra bedroom to me,
and told me;
"That's all I can give."
I lived there,
till my welfare was approved,
then when it went through,
I could only afford an efficiency,
but I had to move.
It was lonely,
not having friends to talk to;
my siblings wouldn't take me out,
because I didn't drink alcohol;
which is what they liked to do.
I never could see anything good,
come from drinking alcohol,
just nice people getting mean,
or drink so much they would fall.

I Think I can

As a child,
I grew up knowing lots of relatives,
I had cousins, aunt and lots of others,
Such as my mom and even brothers.
My brothers have always doubted me,
saying "you'll never be allowed to do that"
In my mind saying we'll see.
They come to my home,
and see projects I have done,
saying no way,
As if they're the only ones.
They doubt my ability,
to do anything well,
then start laughing at me,
And say go to hell.
As I grew up,
my brothers separated from me,
because I was never like them,
And I never want to be.
Because I was born with a disability,
it effected the way they thought of me,
But I won't let it affect my abilities.

CHAPTER 4

❧

I needed to get myself together,
find a barber college,
so I wouldn't have to be,
On assistance forever.
I always liked playing with others hair,
when I seen a barber college,
across the street,
I felt confident about going there.
I asked my only friend,
if he would watch my son,
while I went to school,
I told David other than you;
I don't know anyone.
I felt proud for graduating,
after nine months of school,
but then I wasn't allowed to get a license,
feeling like a loser;
Once again I was fooled.
I applied for jobs,
in bars and restaurants,
but as soon as they seen epilepsy,
on my application;
I wasn't the person they wanted.
It's like society feared me,
because of my epilepsy,
societies response to me seizing,
Was to stand there; and laugh at me.
People thought,
my wild actions on the ground,

was from getting drunk,
when I would come out of it;
I'd tell them I don't drink that junk.
When I would see those people again,
they avoided me,
as if I had some disease,
Thinking they were better than me.

There was a time I had five loving brothers,
I thought I would have someone
to turn to in time of need,
instead of turning to others.
I learned the hard way what each
of them thought of me,
for I wasn't what they each thought I should be.
I just wanted them to love me,
for they were a part of me,
I just wanted them to open their eyes and see.
These poems are written about them individually,
for these are the feelings I felt when
they turned their back on
me
It's not too Late.
When we were younger you
wanted to fit into the crowd
For you to tell them I'm not taking
this anymore; was too
hard.
All you wanted was to have friends,
it didn't matter the cost,
you ended up with nothing in the end,
Everything you once had; you lost.
You got out of prison for the bad things that year,
my kids seen you one time,
now you refuse to contact me;
because of rumors you hear
I still love you no matter what has been done to me,

that will never change,
for the lord has led me,
to a life of eternity.
I hope one day you'll open your cold heart,
and believe in him too,
You continue to live a life of sin,
when our maker comes for those who believe;
What's the words he will say to you.
I hope one day you will come to follow him,
so you can also spend eternity in heaven,
And not in hell for never receiving him.

Greed gets you nowhere

It is better to give than to receive,
people like you don't know what it's like,
To love others, only deceive.
you only go to collect all you can for free,
stealing from others,
Just so you could be happy.
you may have gotten away with it before,
but don't think that when I die,
You're going to get more.
I only buy what I need in order to live,
I have no need to go and buy,
an abundance of things,
For I feel it's better to give.
I feel no need to go and buy things,
I know I can't afford,
for all I need to do,
Is turn it over to the lord.
If I already have what I need,
why would I go out and buy more,
when there's needy people out there,
Who are starving; because they are poor.
Just remember,
greed can kill many things,
even your love for God,
because you refuse to know him;
Because you obsess over new things.
I am rich too with God's love,
for he will supply me with whatever is needed,
All I do is pray to the lord above.

It's A Shame

It's a shame how you use the
hardships from our childhood,
you use them as a an excuse,
instead of helping a homeless person,
Because you think you're too good.
It's a shame you refuse to learn what it's like to love,
you just marry women to get what you can,
Then you flee like a dove.
It's a shame that money means so much to you,
that you won't even help a person,
who's going through hard times,
Yet we lived that way too.
It's a shame you refuse to let
yourself be loved by me,
I was different in your eyes,
therefore the love I had for you,
You wouldn't see.
It's a shame you feel an enormous
amount of jealousy,
if someone has something you don't,
all that can be seen in your eyes,
Is envy.
It's a shame you get mad at me for having what I do,
instead of being proud of me,
you feel I shouldn't have it;
Because I can't work too.

It's a shame the lord says he'll
provide us of our needs,
but that's not good enough for you,
For your heart is filled with greed.

Losing Eternity for a T.V

You feel the world owes you a living,
and you shouldn't have to work,
you watch people for a few days,
then go into a home taking everything they own;
What a jerk.
You feel it's Ok to rob and scare people,
for you don't have a loving bone in your body,
What makes you think your better?
God created all men equal.
You feel your too good to get caught,
one day you will rob the wrong person,
Then and there a hard lesson will be taught.
You feel it's okay to make kids then stray,
you don't believe it's your job to support them,
Then social services come and takes them away.
You feel you have nobody to explain your faults to,
I feel for you when that last day comes,
The maker will take me to heaven,
Where will that leave you.

Forgive them Lord

Forgive them lord,
for they continue to live in a world of sin,
for when that dying man on the
side of the road, needed a
ride;
They blew him off like the wind.
Forgive them Lord,
for they don't love anyone but themselves,
when somebody seeks help from them,
They say ask someone else.
For I was able to forgive this man,
who molested me,
just by saying, I forgive you to him;
Had set two souls free.
Sometimes people never believe in Jesus,
until there's a tragedy,
maybe that's what needs to happen with them,
So they will open their eyes to see.
I know I have sinned in this world too,
but I sought forgiveness from you Lord,
and now I believe in you,
For that is all they have to do.
I hope and pray that one day,
they will seek forgiveness from you,
for if they want to spend eternity in heaven,
That is what they must do.
I just felt like giving up on everything,

for everything I tried just failed,
if society gave me a chance,
They could see that I can do something.
I sat there holding my baby,
just breaking down and crying,
having no way to support him,
I just felt like dying.
My welfare worker told me,
I needed to apply for disability,
I did as I was told,
Waiting for years for them to help me.
An acquaintance of my husbands,
stopped by my house,
I told him roger is no longer here,
then stated to me,
I didn't come to see that louse.
My Ex-husbands friend said
"I came to see if you were ok,
or needed any help,"
I felt like I was swept away.
He asked,
if I needed someone to talk to,
I said yes,
but what could you possibly do,
he said,
"I can take care of you and your baby,
you don't deserve to be abused,
You should be treated like a lady.
Just let me show you what real love is,"

he promised to love me ultimately,
And my baby; as if my child were his.
I asked him,
"So will you flee when you see
a seizure come upon me?
Be like all others in society?"

Judgment Day

Don't judge that person,
for the way they dress,
just because it's not fancy,
doesn't make you more of a person,
In fact; it makes you less.
Don't judge that person,
walking down the road cold and hungry,
for if it happened to you one day,
is that the way;
You would want society to be?
Don't judge that person,
passed out on the sidewalk,
you stand there laughing,
instead of getting help,
For the person; who can't talk.
Don't judge that person,
living next to you,
for they don't have as much as you,
maybe they don't feel the need for it;
Like you.
So when you lose all that fancy stuff,
clothing you used to wear,
remember that person,
while you're asking;
Why doesn't anyone care?
When you find yourself homeless,
for you lost your job,

trying to keep yourself clean;
So you don't feel like a slob.
When a child of yours,
suddenly lose their mobility,
remember that person,
you laughed at on the sidewalk,
while your crying;
Asking why me?
When your house burns down leaving nothing,
remember that person you gawked at,
for having less than you,
now your homeless;
What are you going to do?
Just remember,
the above could happen to you,
so don't judge, lest ye be judged,
As the bible tells us to do.

I was blinded,
by the emotions he showed me,
I just felt in my heart,
That our relationship was meant to be.
We felt it was time to commit to each other,
after making love to me the first time,
I was told my first husbands son,
Would soon have a sister or brother.
I was happy and scared,
fearing would he love his baby,
or leave me,

like my ex husband;
Because he no longer cared.
For he promised to never leave me,
he acted so proud,
and showed off the two babies,
To his friends but; mostly family.
I met his siblings, mother and father,
they showed love towards the kids,
But when it came to him, they didn't bother.
Almost two years passed,
he started being lazy,
he chose drugs and alcohol,
Over the kids and me.
I still stayed with him
for I had a fear of being alone,
yelling at me when he was drunk,
no other man would want you;
That I would spend the rest of my life alone.
he kept promising he would change,
I found out I was pregnant again,
I told him to do something,
Or something will have to be arranged.
He visited the kids during the day,
not knowing,
when coming to my home at nights,
He was taking a part of my body away.
I went to see my obstetrician,
he stated,
"if you haven't been sexually active,

Then how did you become pregnant again."
I went through this, for four years,
doing sit-ups to abort fetuses,
Guilt and hurt inside me; while crying my tears.
I didn't have any friends,
to help me escape,
and I knew if I stayed,
he would keep committing;
The act of rape.
then went bragging,
about how he took my body,
while I was asleep,
once again a man lied about promises;
He failed to keep.
I filed a restraining order on him,
telling myself,
they are all the same,
that's not the kind of male;
I want to be with.

After the state provided my kids and I with welfare,
I no longer feared leaving him,
I could afford to pay my rent,
So I didn't need him there. My
friend heard I was by myself,
so he kept checking to see if I needed anything,
And to make sure I was still good with my health.

Taking Without Asking

When I started dating you, I thought
I found my soul mate,
then you broke your promises, and
took a part of my body
every night,
you created so much hate.
You and I created this little boy,
and for months after he was born
he was your wondrous joy.
We didn't want more children now,
we used protection when making love,
but when I went for my check-up,
and was told I'm pregnant;
I said how.
You wanted it whether I did or not,
you would wait for my pills to
knock me out, come in at
night,
Telling yourself I'll just take what she got.
You found your pleasure in taking sex from me,
knowing the end result, would be a baby.
When I told you I was leaving you threatened me,
I'll find out where you are, then I'll take the babies.
he said leave and I'll kill you,
now it's been seven years the kids
are alive and happy too.

CHAPTER 5

৵৹

After feeling destroyed by the men in my past,
I searched myself, seeking out that
wrong thing in all them,
that didn't allow them to last.
I felt like men were all the same,
they play with my feelings, take
what they want, then dump
you;
Like it's a game.
I was scared of feeling lonely all my life,
I only felt hatred for men, asking
myself, how will I ever
become a wife.
I had three children, nobody to turn to,
donating blood illegally to feed them,
There was nothing else I could do.
My mom said "come to bingo with
me; you need to get out of
the house for a while,"
that's where I met this guy.
After seeing him a few times at bingo,
he approached me, asking me, "do
you mind if I sit here;" I
said "no."
He talked about Vietnam, while
the man called the numbers
out,
half the time I couldn't understand
what he was talking

about.
When bingo was through,
he walked outside with me, before
shutting the car door,
He asked; "will you go out on a date with me."
I couldn't give him an answer there and then,
for I sensed something strange in him,
I'd never seen in other men.
Even though he was a disabled veteran,
He still worked as an appliance repairman.
and was still getting divorced from his wife,
So I was leery, of letting another
man into my kids life.
I had respect for him for fighting for our country,
I just didn't understand what a
52-year-old would see in me.
I was only 32 at the time,
yet I felt useless because society
wouldn't view the abilities of
mine.
I felt no man could ever love me,
with having three children and a disability.
I had no knowledge for any type of job,
I felt if I didn't get with some man,
I'd end up with a slob.
I didn't get much when I went to the blood bank,
My kids got angry at me, I'd say
you have your dad's to
thank.

Loving Son Disappears

I remember being sixteen,
almost ready to give birth to you,
I felt so much hatred towards your dad,
I was scared; I wouldn't be able to love you.
Then they brought in this nine pound
ten ounce baby to me, all
I could feel, was an enormous amount of love;
For my little baby.
You never got the chance to meet
your dad, but that didn't
matter to you and I, as long as we
had each other, we were
glad.
As you had gotten older,
you seen something wrong with mommy,
you seen me pass out, and drop to the floor,
But when I woke up; you were right beside me.
You wasn't ashamed of it, or
scared to be around me,
I would wake up, and you would say,
It's okay; just rest mommy.
You were thankful for all you received,
just to have food every day, was a blessing,
There was no room for greed.
I now see the boy I had given birth to,
now you say you're scared of me,
and no longer want to see me,

Lord what did I do?
You now blame me, for your real
dad not wanting you,
you say he would have quit with the abuse,
If I would have done what I was supposed to.
I will love you till my dying day,
you can run and live in denial,
But my love for you, is one thing
you can't take away.
I felt there was no use for me being here,
I didn't like myself or men either,
For all I got from them was fear.
I kept convincing myself that he wasn't the same,
just able to see the good in him,
like a kid; playing a game.
Laying in bed at nights by myself, crying
fearing loneliness all my life,
nobody to love; I just felt like dying.
Nobody seemed interested in me,
so I when I went out to dance,
yet it's like nobody seen me.
I started panicking, about never being a wife,
so I told him yes, not realizing
I wouldn't have a life.
I hoped to have that wedding all women dream of,
he said, I can't afford that;
I have kids to take care of. My
third husband had me move
into his home with him,

Since he owned it, and didn't want
to make payments again.
I knew I wasn't some great looking female,
for each man I had been with in
the past, ended up in jail.
my husband was older than others in the past,
I assumed he was wiser, and not so stupid,
therefore the relationship would last.
I was thirty-two he was fifty-two,
he went out with his kids, he was charming too.
After we married he quit taking me out,
like he use to, I found myself asking him,
what's this all about? I found
myself doing things in the
home,
when I asked if he would help, he said "I can't,
because of my amputated leg;"
so I did it alone. Because of my disorders,
I had to have things to do,
since I was the only one doing these things,
there was no me and you.
After that he quit spending time with the children,
telling myself here we go again.
After being abused by the men in my past,
I took martial arts so if any man
hit me, it would be his last.
When I had a seizure, He would pin me down,
instead of letting it take its course,
And move anything that was around.

He had three kids too,
and when he pinned me while seizing,
kids of mine would yell,
"Mom he's going to hurt you."
When I went to my neurologist,
and he seen the bruises on my body,
He told my spouse; to stop doing that
I walked my kid's school down the street,
people stared at the bruises on my body,
I felt I needed to go to karate;
So he could no longer abuse me.

Lessons In life

Karate is a way of challenging
myself, it's a large part of my
life, and improves my health.
Karate is like having a second life, I can work out,
Care for my children; and still be a good wife.
Karate has given me back my self esteem,
now I'm able to tell myself I can,
And it doesn't have just been a dream.
There will always be challenges,
and decisions to make,
some will be hard, and even bad but,
It's the chance I'll have to take.
I've walked out of class being swung at
or even hit, leaving a lasting mark on me,
Just to see others gawk at it.
I no longer have to hide my body from my family,
when it's discolored, or even bruised,
now it's from taking self defense class,
And not from being abused.
Karate was a sport I always wanted to learn,
Providing great exercises, learning
which way to turn.
Since I have joined karate and gotten into class,
I now can walk my line, and don't
have to watch it pass.
I don't sit on the side anymore

Waiting to be called to go and do
the activity on the floor.
In karate we all stand in one line,
people on both sides of you,
But no one is behind.
All are treated equally in class,
because we all go there to learn,
And we don't just get passed.
Karate has helped me education wise,
so now I can see where others come from,
Not just what I see in my eyes.
For several months, there was a kick I tried to learn,
asking myself how hard can it be,
All you need to do is jump and turn.
After several classes I went home crying,
because I didn't accomplish the round house,
Was I trying?
I would look around in class as
I waited for my teacher,
watching others do it,
Asking myself why can't I do it too.
I think of the movements of this kick,
like a train, one move lines up with the next,
Putting it into place; is a talent of the brain.
The spinning crescent kick is used in kotta's,
and many techniques,
I have been given the ability to use it,
And I feel it's very unique.
By getting educated on a project,

and following it through,
gave my brain the ability,
To say I can do it too.
I have lost allot of brain cells,
some help me to remember,
Others it hard to tell.
I need to exercise and work with
what I got,
so that little bit I once remembered,
Will soon be allot.
I have the need to repeat things over and over,
to be able to store it in my brain,
and be able to perform them,
When called out by name.
I need to practice my techniques every day,
So I don't forget them, and let them slip away.
Karate I now can attend,
and I no longer need my doctors permission,
Therefore there's no reason for other's to offend.
For if I don't do my techniques every day,
it's like a kid going to school,
The very first day,
I then have to learn it all,
all over again as if I was never shown
Except now I have to relearn it on my own.
There's no way to explain the benefits,
of this martial art,
there's also no way it can be taken from me,
For it will always be in my heart.

My stepdaughter confided in me,
instead of her dad,
she was scared of talking to him,
She knew he would get mad.
His son never liked me,
for having another female in the house,
besides his mom, was the last thing,
He wanted to see.

Neither of my sons liked my husband's boy,
I couldn't figure out,
why they hated him
I found out; he was playing with them like a toy.
My stepdaughter asked me if I
go for a walk with her,
She told me she might be pregnant, but I'm not sure.
She asked me please don't tell dad,
He couldn't have any more kids,
So when he seen the results he was
mad. He started yelling
and throwing things,
Screaming at her; do ya know what this means.
After this event happened to the
family, my daughter started
rebelling against me.
I was trying my best to be a good mom,
then my daughter said,
"you never have time for me;
You're always gone." I told her
"nobody can ever take your place,"
when the doctor said it's a girl,
I had the biggest smile on my face.
I couldn't believe,
how quick my life was changed,
It's like my husband had it arranged.
There was this man who was charming,
not even two months later, he became violent,
Not caring who he was harming.

These friends of ours from karate,
came every weekend,
to play dungeons and dragons,
They never seen that side of him like me.
Weekdays I did stuff just to stay busy,
so at the end of the day,
I didn't have to listen to him;
Complain about me.
Other than karate,
I had no life outside the home,
so when I needed someone to talk to,
I was alone.
I looked at a picture,
of my husband and me on the wall,
asking myself,
how much do I love him;
Answer being nothing at all.
I decided on that day,
I needed to find someone, to help me get away.
After karate was over the next
day, I asked Steve can you
help me? It's like he was willing,
until I said I have epilepsy.

Making Believe

There are special people
that others call friends, I've always wanted one,
But it always seemed to end.
My children asked me, mom how
come you don't do things
with others,
But all I had was my brothers.
Why do these people,
I look to as a friend,
shy away, is it something I do;
Or something I say.
I looked at you as one these people,
known as a friend,
I told you secrets of me,
Then it just seemed to end.
Had I not told you these secrets of me,
would you still like me,
Would you feel differently?
Does it make you uncomfortable,
knowing of my past,
or can we have a friendship,
One that will last.

The following weekend,
Steve and my care provider came over to play,
I asked my care provider for help,
I told him I had epilepsy;

He helped me anyway.
A couple days later,
my child's school called me,
There's something you need to hear; and see.
A police officer, and social worker was there,
my child said, he touched me;
I asked when and where.
I told her don't worry,
it won't happen again,
were leaving,
I just need to get ahold of my friend.

Secrets That Kill

A partner is who stands by your side,
goes through the ups and downs with you,
Like a carnival ride.
You'll have bad times, and good
times too, picking each
other up, when the other falls; is what partners do.
Partners don't keep secrets from each other,
they're willing to share events or happenings,
Like what ya did with your sister or mother.
What you speak, is either the truth or a lie,
honesty may hurt, but to fib hurts worse;
Like you want to die.
The pain from the truth eventually goes away,
When you lie, it takes trust away,
along with not knowing;
what to say.
Partners trust each other,
with their body and soul,
never having to wonder,
In seventy years; will I still be whole.

Men

When it comes to the men,
I've been with in the past,
I haven't had anything,
But bad luck trying to make them last.
I got married at fifteen years of age,
not because I loved the man,
But to free myself from being caged.
I didn't know what love felt like yet,
so when he cheated on me,
He wasn't hard to forget.
I suffered no love loss,
but loss of self esteem,
feeling to have a man forever;
Is only in dreams.
I fell in love at the age sixteen,
he was all women dream of,
it's like he was sent,
From God above.
I married him,
when he asked me to,
regretting that,
after seeing myself;
Black and blue.
Do I accept this as life,
is this what it's like,
To be a wife.
After years of being alone,

I started feeling scared,
fearing no man wanted me,
Not one who cared.
I felt a strange love,
for this man I met,
there were things,
different about him,
but I figured;
He was all I would ever get.
He wasn't abusive,
and didn't believe in cheating,
so I wasn't worried,
About taking a beating.
When being asked to marry him,
once again I said yes,
not knowing three years later,
this faded love;
Would turn into a mess.
I tried to figure him out,
what was I attracted to,
Nothing is all that came out.
I find myself asking,
Are all men the same?
they play with you,
until they're bored,
then trade you for another;
Like it's a game.
When I look at the man,
I know as my friend, and lover,

it's impossible to imagine myself;
With any other.
I never thought a good looking man,
would be interested in me,
because of having three children;
And my disability.
I get encouragement,
and self-esteem from my friend,
re-assuring me, he'll stand by my side;
Till the end.
It's unexplainable,
the way he makes my insides feel,
It's a beautiful feeling within me,
Telling myself it has to be real.
My children look up to this man,
I speak of,
because they see a male,
who doesn't have to scream;
To show them love.
The love I feel for him,
is so deep and strong,
to have it taken away,
would leave me asking;
Now what did I do wrong?
I wouldn't have it in me,
to love another man,
after failing love so many times,
I couldn't again say; I think I can.

If for some reason,
his love for me disappears,
I ask God to take me,
So I need not; cry anymore tears.

CHAPTER 6

❧

After getting things into
my care provider's place,
I told him,
"when it comes to my body,
don't expect anything;"
While staring into his face.
I felt like,
I was going to go crazy,
I just couldn't handle anymore,
Mentally.

Why Am I Here

A house full of people,
making different sounds,
yet it's so lonely,
as if there were;
No one around.
One playing with a friend,
one is whining the other is snoring,
wishing my life;
Wasn't so boring.
Being restricted,
from going to places,
seeing new things;
And new faces.
Having to stay indoors,
because of the sun,
What kind of life is that?
not one with activity,
And it sure isn't fun.
You see other's,
with your same condition,
yet they're not limited,
It's like being on restriction.
If you're not able, to go outside
and explore,
meet other's,
and associate;
Then what am I here for?

Only having one person,
to take me somewhere,
having to feel guilty,
for taking their time,
it's almost not worth it;
Like why should I care.

My care provider say's "I'm here,
if you need someone to talk to,"
I asked him, "where am I going to go?
I have nobody to turn to."
My care provider had medical training,
from the military,
so when I seized,
He assured me not to worry.
Several times while having a seizure,
he would tell others,
just get out of the way,
I can take care of her.
I wouldn't trade my care provider,
My Pastor's daughter, and my doctor
for anything, together they
kept up;
On the newest things.

The Healing Hands

I give the staff who worked with me,
a special thanks,
to all who helped me,
Even when I got belligerent; or angry.
This is to all of you,
who chose medical as your profession,
for you help those who get hurt,
from each event;
You learn a lesson.
I wanted to be a barber,
or a nurse, the state said I couldn't,
because of my seizure's;
And that was the worst.
I learned what the Lord wanted me to do,
to reach out to others,
That are going through; the same trials too.
Written to all the staff at Neurology Consultants.

When I lived with my care provider,
he wasn't in a relationship at the time,
for his luck in making them last,
Was like mine.
My care provider had his own
life, he would come home
with his beer, watch TV,
I'd be cleaning;
Going out of my mind.
This man that came home every night,
never yelling, getting violent,
seemed to good to be true.
Like something wasn't right.
When new problems for me,
came up,
he always offered to talk about them,
but when it came to him expressing his,
He would close up.
I started having feelings of love,
for this guy,
but kept them hidden,
I didn't know,
if he was interested in me;
Or if they were forbidden.
My care provider told me he had a son,
he would never again see.
that he cared for him.
while his mom served in the first gulf war;
Because My care provider left the military.

My care provider was an alcoholic at that time,
when my care provider's wife returned,
she wanted a divorce,
she no longer wanted her life;
To be a part of mine.
My care provider and his wife, parted as friends,
no hatred between them,
Which wasn't usually the way, a marriage ends.
I couldn't understand,
why my care provider would choose alcohol,
over a friend,
alcohol brought his marriage;
To an end.
I knew alcohol wasn't a good thing,
I seen violence caused from it,
so what was I seeing,
that was so special;
In this human being.
Asking myself,
if I get involved with this man,
would our relationship mean less,
than that can of alcohol,
He holds in his hand.
I had been soul searching, for two years,
I only wanted a man I could love,
doing the same in return,
To longer live these fears.
My daughter asked me,
if I was going to stay with my care provider,

expressing how she felt about him,
I told her; I feel the same way.
I told my daughter that's what's scary,
My care provider might be my soul-mate,
that one day would come;
And then would marry.
Years passing by,
asking my care provider all the time,
when will I see the real you,
I'll be this way; till I die.
My physician notified me,
about a device,
that might help my condition,
thinking that would be nice
He told me,
it's called A Vagus Nerve Stimulator,
I was seizing every week,
To me anything is better.

Partners Looking For A Cure

I Have had this condition epilepsy,
since I was three,
a doctor would quit that practice,
then find another;
That would accept me.
Always getting medicines changed,
because one didn't agree with another,
Leaving me feeling strange.
A doctor,
who treated me for years,
told me he's retiring,
what about the medicines;
For my seizures.
I called my insurance company,
one of them, only seen children,
But the other accepted me.
Doctor Brian My doctor has seen me,
for almost twenty years,
his goal has always been,
not to have any every month;
With my seizures.
Every three months, he asked me,
any seizures, I'd say yes,
The goal; is to not have any.
Dr. My doctor
has always been an inspiration to me,
always saying,

I'll get you to zero a month,
You wait and see.
My Pastor's daughter would call me back,
and do what the nurses do,
she showed love from her heart,
Making sure nothing was wrong with you.
I'd call her two or three times a day,
of side effects I was feeling,
She responded right away.
I' have to call at nine or ten at night,
the nurse telling me, My doctor's on call
I need him to call me;
Something isn't right.
He would call right away,
never got upset
because it was so late,
Or ask why didn't you call earlier today.
My doctor and my Pastor's daughter,
this is to thank you,
for committing yourselves,
To all who need you.
For you both gave time,
to research things,
like the implant inside me,
so I could keep my mobility;
And be a human being.
For I will never forget,
the two of you,
you gave me inspiration,
To do what others; said I'd never do.

Doctor My doctor,
devoted his time to study neurology,
his office received a call from Denver,
about an implant,
That might help others; and me.
My doctor asked,
if I was willing to have it put in me,
on a trial basis,
I told him,
"Anything is better than this."
I need something,
besides medicine,
for at that time,
I'd been tried, on all of them.
My doctor said "Remember,
this is only a trial basis,
to see if it will work;"
On conditions like this.
It was time to see My doctor,
for my three month visit,
I seen what it looked like,
He showed me how to operate it.
My doctor explained,
that it ran off a battery,
that lasted five to seven years,
surgeons would replace it;
Doing the same surgery.
When they first implanted it in me,
they implanted it underneath my armpit,

weeks after the surgery,
It slipped.
I told my doctor,
I wanted it placed on my chest,
whether other women wore it there or not,
For I wasn't vain, like the rest.
My body started to seize,
My care provider used the magnet device,
it didn't respond,
Oh great; isn't this nice.
I said to my doctor,
"I thought this was such a great device?
first it slips,
then the battery dies,"
I've had surgery twice.
Doctor's constantly contacting the company,
telling them,
to get a new one,
And make sure; it has a good battery.
In the summer time,
I wore only tank tops,
when I went shopping,
people that walked fast;
Suddenly came to a stop.

The Implant That Gives Me Life

It's been eight years,
since the creation of this implant,
it could help many live longer,
So they could say I can; not I can't.
I talk to others,
with my same condition,
yet never heard of this device,
therefore they live a life;
Of restriction.
Two of my children have epilepsy,
my son and I, wanted less seizures,
So we had the surgery.
My son used to seize every night,
now he maybe has one a year,
What could be more right.
I used to have three,
or four guaranteed,
after giving the implant to me,
now thirty to ninety days;
I feel so lucky.
Why aren't neurologists allowed
to tell society,
about this device,
epileptics becoming seizure free,
That would be nice.
This device is called,
a Vagus nerve stimulator,

what right do others have,
To make a person's; life span shorter.
It costs forty thousand dollars,
for this device,
yet others say,
That life; isn't worth a price.
So money,
means more than a life,
I bet they wouldn't be so restrictful,
If it was their family, like their wife.
Written by Nicole
My care provider didn't have much experience,
in raising children,
leaving me to wonder,
would he love my kids,
Or turn away from them.
My daughter looked up to my care provider,
wanted him to just be a dad,
she didn't know the words,
to show the feelings towards him;
She had.
She said.
I want him to be my daddy,
to teach me, love me,
And not run away from me,
she brought a book home one day,
she had asked me,
"do you think he'll read it,
Or throw it away."

The book was reasons
a daughter needs a dad,
when my care provider read it,
and she seen on his face,
Then she was glad.
She asked my care provider,
if she could call him dad,
he said if you want to,
she now had something,
She never had.
After seeing my care provider's reaction,
I kept trying to convince myself,
He was the one.
My care provider showed curiosity,
about my condition,
he would ask questions,
every three months,
when he took me;
To see my physician.
My care provider had done so much for me,
I wasn't thankful for things,
he wasn't obligated to do;
Hatred was all I could see.
From the types of damages,
done to me, blinding me,
feeling they're all the same,
My care provider showed me he cared;
Then I was able to see.
I was usually expressing anger,

when my care provider came home,
for the duration of two years,
Cursing, because of feeling alone.
One day after my care provider went to work,
and the kids went to school,
I wrote a note to my care provider,
crying the whole time;
Feeling like a fool.
When I read it,
to check for mistakes,
I realized it was in poetry form,
Letting go of the hatred; is all it takes.
My care provider was still at work,
so I put it on his pillow,
he got home and read it,
then came to me saying;
"I feel the same way also."
Afterwards I told the children.
My care provider and I want to be together,
my son's sighed,
My daughter asked; will it be forever.
After we were alone the first night,
he would be my last,
for the love I'd had for his,
It couldn't have felt more right.
I told my care provider he'd probably
never meet my family,
as you've seen for several years,
They've had nothing to do with me.

My care provider said
reach out to them,
if they turn away from you,
or hang the phone up,
They're not ready; to make amends.

Running Scared

Why do people who say they love you,
find it so difficult to be with you,
during your last days,
knowing at any time;
It can be taken away.
Your own child is scared,
to come and see you,
for if you have a seizure
They don't know what to do.
Your mother refuses to face reality,
week after week goes by
Taking more of her daughter's abilities.
Your brother's abandon you,
because of embarrassment or shame,
not wanting to be around you,
Who's really to blame?
I really feel for you all,
all knowing who I speak of,
because you don't know what it's like,
To be receiving Gods love.
I don't have a fear of dying,
for I have faced reality,
for when the Lord takes me,
Why can't you be happy for me?
For your only think of yourselves,
and about what you'll lose,
But what did you feel for me?

nothing you cared more;
About you're booze.
I'm sorry,
you couldn't love me for who I was,
but I still leave this world loving you,
that's the way God,
wants me to leave this world;
And me too.

CHAPTER 7

❧

My older son liked my care provider,
and thought he was cool,
until my care provider started enforcing rules,
And one of those was to go to school.
He could handle being my care provider's friend,
but when my care provider and I became one,
anger came out of him,
For his power; came to an end.
my daughter asked me one day,
"why does dad drink that stinky stuff,"
she said, "I'm going to ask;
When he comes home today."
I told her,
when your dad kisses me,
I hold my breath,
Because I think it's stinky.
Every day my care provider came home,
walking in with his beer,
maybe that's his way,
Of feeling he's not alone.
Asking myself if I can't get
him to give up something that's stinky,
Where would there be room, in his life for me.
When my care provider came home that day,
he headed to the kitchen,
To put his brew away. Our daughter
had asked her daddy,
"how can you drink something,
So stinky."

Both of them looking at each other,
My care provider said "Hang tight,
    while I go to the store."
When he returned he had another.
My care provider opened one up, handing it to her,
    she said I can't stand the smell,
    Makes me want to throw up.
My care provider kept handing the cans to her,
    till they were gone, she then asked,
"Does this mean your quitting daddy."
    I'd been trying to get my care
    provider to quit for years,
    my daughter came and hugged me,
    While crying out the tears.

My Dream

I can't put into words,
the way you make me feel,
it's so intense and beautiful,
I get scared, I'll wake up and see;
It's not real.
The way I feel for you,
I've never felt before,
just tell me,
you refuse to let yourself be loved;
And I'll walk out the door.
Sometimes after a conversation ends,
on the phone,
I no longer hear you say,
I love you,
Thinking one day; I'll be alone.
When we go out to dance,
you make me feel like we're in heaven,
because it's all there,
So I tell myself; here's your chance.
If I'm feeling down or something's wrong,
you ask me to tell you about it,
So I open up to you, once again I feel strong.
If you have problems,
you won't open up to me,
it's like it's one sided,
That's not the way it's supposed to be.
I am here for you,

through the good and the bad,
I want to be your partner for life,
For the happy and sad.
I've always believed,
that's what makes couples stronger,
going through trials together,
forming bonds,
making the relationship;
Last longer.
I'm not with you,
because I have to be,
I'm with you,
because I love you,
The beautiful feeling; you have given me.
So when will you believe me when I say,
"my love won't end"
that I am here forever,
As your lover; and your friend.
Because of others,
you've been with in the past,
are you not able to trust women,
Does it mean; this relationship won't last.
I don't see you,
as other men I've been with before,
you know how to give the feeling of love,
And so much more.
You've asked me several times before,
Why me, when you could have, so much more.
Maybe I could have money,

or a new car,
but those won't give the feel of love,
Like I have in my heart.
With you I want to grow old,
and spend the rest of my life,
in hopes,
one day you'll feel this way too;
And then become your wife.

From the time,
I moved in with my care provider,
through the time we bought the condo,
he would tell me,
Give it to the Lord; let it go.
I learned allot from my care provider,
why stress over problems,
that was causing me to seize,
If there's nothing you can do.
When my kids got in trouble,
I always felt guilty,
for I couldn't give them,
What others had; a good family.

My 4 Best Friends

Mom I want you and dad to
know, your special to me,
You taught me things about myself, I couldn't see.
4 you, dad and my care provider
showed me God loved me too.
Be my best and do what God would have me do.
Everybody that person to turn to,
So I felt special, because I had two.
The two of you never pushed me away,
For that reason, I became who I am today.
Realizing form words spoken by the three of you,
I learned to trust again, so I could
love my care provider.
Each of you are special to me,
Now I have a mom, dad and best
friend; and god loves me
too
Don't forget each of you helped me
get to where I am today,
So don't hurt for me, be happy, I'll
see you again someday.
My care provider's father had spoke about,
hard times he had,
trying to provide for his family,
sometimes working two jobs;
When it eased up he was glad.

My care provider's mother stood by
my care provider's father's side,
no matter whether
The road was narrow or wide.
My care provider's father and my
care provider's mother,
invited us to their home,
in the country,
My care provider told me what they were like,
thinking;
They're not going to like me.
I even cursed in their home,
My care provider's father suddenly spoke,
in an unusual tone,
to not use that language;
In his home.
I didn't get up and walk away,
because after listening to it,
I asked myself do I want my kids;
To talk this way.

A Mom

I've searched for thirty four years,
for this female image I hold in my mind,
always feeling,
There was no such woman; of this kind.
I promised myself,
to never trust another female,
because of the end result,
The act of betrayal.
I've know this woman,
less than two years,
yet shared more with her,
than the lady,
Who should have wiped away; my tears.
This woman I speak of is you,
what once was only an image,
You have allowed to come true.
I love you for being the woman,
that stood by my side,
instead of running away,
Saying, oh well I tried.
Any female can be a mother,
but it takes a special woman like you,
To be the other.
You have made my dreams,
completely true,
not only did I find my significant other,
But God gave me; a mom too.

A Dad

Special characteristics of this image,
only existed in my mind,
then I met you,
once again hearing myself saying,
There is another one of his kind.
Never expecting to see this image again,
I wasn't prepared, to see a man,
with those characteristics,
I found myself saying to my care
provider; I'm scared.
I may do things,
you don't fully approve of,
though I feel,
you would be there to pick me up,
That's what I call love.
You give suggestions,
of things I should do,
but you don't talk down to me,
If I fail, then say shame on you.
Men like you are few and far between,
always reaching out to others,
expecting nothing in return;
Is hardly ever seen.
You had to handle the hard times,
as well as the good,
but you held your family together,
Like only a dad could.

I think my father would be proud,
looking at you,
seeing the kind of man you are,
he would know my dream;
Had come true.
You are a man,
any girl would be proud to call dad,
it took twenty seven years,
but now I have something,
For years I never had; a dad.

My care provider's father would talk to me,
when I needed advice,
when my son would get violent,
warning him to quit hitting his sibling;
Or pay the price.
My son never took me,
or other females seriously,
for he started showing,
More and more disrespect to me.
I would ask my care provider,
"what did I do wrong,
that he treats me so bad,"
I cared for him on my own,
For so long.
I folded my hands,
when going to bed,
Asking God lead me,
what is it I'm suppose to do;
I don't understand.
I had allot of respect for my care provider's father,
so when he gave advice,
I'd use it to teach my kids,
Yet the end result wasn't nice.

Innocence Dies

I had this toddler,
full of innocence and cries,
every year as he got older,
he got filled with guilt;
And lots of lies.
For several years,
my child and I were very poor,
as long as there was love in our house,
We needed nothing more.
You would watch over me,
every day every hour,
not because you cared or loved me,
fearing a man;
Would take away you power.
You quit being thankful,
for what you had received,
always wanting something more,
feeling I should buy it for you,
For this is what you believed.
At the age of nine,
my little boy died,
no longer caring,
about what I was feeling,
no longer asking me;
what's wrong when I cried,
You have become deviant and wild,
you could care less,

whether I'm dead or alive,
That's not my child.
I hope you find this person,
you call your dad,
beating people up,
Making them feel sad.
If you ever grow up,
and become a man,
just remember it wasn't me,
That said, I don't think I can.
I've waited for seven years,
for my boy to return,
after not seeing any results,
I know he's dead;
And so are my fears.

I Stand alone

There are three others here,
other than me, finding myself alone,
nobody to confide in,
Asking myself how can it be.
Having this hurt inside,
because others abandoned me,
asking God,
what's wrong with me,
to make my siblings;
No longer love me.
I didn't repeat things,
other's had done,
staying by my kids side,
donating blood to feed them,
but when it comes,
To being wrong; I'm the one.
Seldom hearing thank you,
for the good I'd done,
only pitiful me,
As if they're; the only one.
Never appreciating things,
done anymore,
because they expect it,
As if it's my chore.
You cook meals,
and keep the house clean,
nobody acknowledges it,

only hearing, what else should be done;
That's mean.
Hearing I love you mostly at night,
when your husband is intimate,
telling myself,
At least I can still do this right.
It seemed like,
I could please him,
one way,
he gets what he wants,
Then rolls away.
Your children going to bed,
without thanking the lord,
just saying what they want,
even when they knew;
It's nothing I could afford.
Saying words of disrespect to you,
for they didn't get their way,
telling them, I've heard it before,
It's just another day.
As I stand here asking God
"who's really by my side"
nobody just comes out,
For all the above had lied.

Love Conquers All

I starved myself,
during my teenage years,
people calling me miss piggy,
When I got home; I'd shed tears.
Wanting to be as skinny,
as the other girls one day,
wishing my fat,
Would melt away.
I would skip meals,
yet I kept getting fatter,
telling others, I'll be the one;
Living happily ever after.
One day people will see,
when turning pages,
in model magazines,
There's the place; you'll see me.
After everyone got their food,
and left the kitchen,
I'd go to the trash; and start pitching.
I'd take trash sitting on the floor,
place it over, the food I threw away,
So it couldn't be seen anymore.
Some of my family,
called me blubber butt,
throwing up all my food,
Leaving nothing; in my gut.
Starving myself and throwing up,

What good did it do?
those people are gone,
And my stomach lining too.
The anorexia never goes away,
I still don't like my body,
When I look in the mirror today.
It's easier to fight it today,
because my care provider hides the scale,
So I don't weigh myself every day.
I have kids that look up to me,
if I throw-up every time I eat,
What kind of teacher would I be?
I just can't think, about what I look like,
I have my daughter,
And my son.

My care provider constantly saying,
just turn it over to the Lord,
I found out was dying,
the fear of seeing Satan;
I couldn't afford.
Asking my care provider,
what will happen, to my children,
two of them,
are always in trouble,
Nobody's going to want them.
I went to bed every night,
fearing not seeing the next day,
Constantly living in fright.

My care provider told me
about this church,
it was in the country,
I asked him, why should I go?
So they can judge me.
So they can say how bad,
my parenting skills were,
My care provider said, "they're not like that,
they're every day people;"
I said "sure."
My care provider said "okay, if you don't like it,
when we walk in,
we'll leave,
and I won't ask you;
To go again."
My care provider said,
"you don't have to wear a dress,
because you're a lady,
most of them wear jeans,
so they can sit through the sermon;
Comfortably."
I agreed to go to this church,
even though it was forty miles away,
That was the best thing,
I did in years,
it's like the world was lifted,
From my shoulders; that day.
My care provider's parents were there that night,
when I seen them,

I was nervous, he assured me;
It will be all right.
Not all my children,
felt the need to keep going,
I'd elbow my son, to wake up,
Because he was snoring.
After the services were over, one night,
I asked my Pastor,
to talk to me,
the feelings from my past;
Didn't feel right.

Nobody's Perfect

I talked to my Pastor one night,
asking if GOD is real,
how come everything I do,
Never turns out right.
I told him,
about my horrific childhood,
then said to me,
Your still here aren't you?
Well that's good.
I told my Pastor,
I feel dirty and nasty,
GOD still loves you,
it was done to me;
Not by me.
I told him words,
a preacher said on Sunday,
I had a child out of wedlock,
so my chance of going to heaven;
Was taken away.
These false words were told to me,
by a catholic preacher,
making words from the bible say,
what he wanted;
Instead of being a teacher.
My care provider and Dad,
showed me statements,
in the bible that were true,

then I wanted to go to church;
And there I met you.
You stood strong and tall,
preaching words of the Lord,
hoping to reach any person,
While other spirits soared.
You didn't condemn me
for the wrongs in my life,
you said give it to the lord,
So you can be a mother; and wife.
God has our lives planned out.
you'll have happy times,
you'll have sad one too,
Making you want to; scream and shout.
If everybody were perfect on earth,
we wouldn't need God for anything,
So what would he be worth?

CHAPTER 8

৩৽৵

We finally paid off, our condominium,
then we decide to move,
my son started yelling,
You can't take away my friends.
The profits from selling it,
was used to open,
a computer game store,
hoping to expand it;
So my care provider could bring in more.
Computer games,
was what he got into,
to keep people coming in,
as soon as one left,
Is what he wanted to do?
To advertise his gaming business
on T.V, so others would learn of it,
And come there to see.
My care provider had a friend,
who was a computer geek
My care provider asked his friend,
to build his machines,
So they could open; within a week.
My daughter had the hot's,
For my care provider's employee,
she was only sixteen,
He was thirty-three.
The employee kept saying,
"I'll take care of Nicole,
just emancipate her,

So she can marry me."
The employee stayed angry, at
my care provider and me,
every month, it made less money,
My care provider said, we have to close honey.
Every night,
after closing the game store,
I went to visit my dying brother,
he was weaker,
And parts of him were sore.
There were two songs, playing on the radio,
when my care provider took me to see My brother,
Or when it was time to go.
The cancer was spread.
throughout my brothers body,
asking God, who's the next one,
You take away from me.
My brother feared, all would just forget him,
I play those songs every month,
That's my way; of remembering him again.
I cry,
every time I hear those songs,
feeling him when I seize,
Asking him, to take me along.
My mother cared for My brother,
again having to watch a child of hers die,
Is nothing; anyone would like.
My brother said,
"my mind and body are fading fast,

I need to do something,
I should have done in the past."
He asked me to call my pastor,
I asked my Pastor to come to him,
My brother knew,
We wouldn't see each other again.
It was very late at night,
when I called pastor my Pastor,
I told him My brother's ready,
and wants' you to come;
So he can be saved.
I'd sit and stroke My brother's face,
I was sad and happy,
for now he's ready,
To go to that other place.
The mirral of angels, I painted for My brother,
had take so long,
only the angels foot was left,
The phone rang; a voice said he's gone.

God Hears All

I go to church, to hear the word of God,
spoken to me,
to teach others and myself,
how to become the kind of person,
The lord wants us to be.
I believe we should help all,
to the best of our ability,
even a stranger, or someone who;
May not like me.
We should apply,
all were capable of,
for that's a way, of showing God;
Were thankful for his love.
God shows us all which path to take,
the choices we make,
determines if it was the right way;
Or a mistake.
For years,
I felt that God didn't love me,
for I'd follow that road, he'd have me take,
the end of the road is tragedy,
Where did I make a mistake.
For several months,
I visited my dying brother,
asking God, don't make him,
Live through another.
I hurt inside,

I can't run my fingers though his hair,
yet I'm relieved he feels no more pain,
He's watching us from up there.
As we remember My son on this day,
be happy for him, for our maker,
Has taken him away.
I'll see My son another day,
we accepted the lord, as our savior,
we'll both enter the kingdom of heaven;
Nobody can take that away.

I looked out the window,
at my care provider's game shop,
suddenly I felt,
Like the world just stopped.

The Good That Comes From Bad #1

I couldn't handle the stress,
of being treated differently,
just for being the person,
God created me to be.
I picked a career that was fun to do,
for I wanted to feel good about myself
And make you proud of me too.
You emancipated me at fifteen,
for that I'm glad,
or I would be where I am today,
And wouldn't have seen what I had.
I don't look at trials as a bad thing,
it made who I am today,
A decent and understanding human being.
I'm glad I didn't have,
what all other kids had,
I appreciate what I have today,
For that I'm glad.
I want you to know I'm proud of you,
You should also be proud of yourself,
For you have overcome trials too.
For you just don't see them yet,
you feel ashamed of it,
so you try to forget,
you beat the alcohol;
What's not to be proud of?
Now you are able to give
and feel the feeling of love,

What's not to be proud of?
Just one seizure,
is enough to kill you,
so when I had six,
I told my husband;
There's something I have to do.
You arrived,
at my husband's gaming place,
nothing but fear within me,
not knowing if;
I'd ever again see your face.
I prayed to God,
please show me what to do,
Next thing I know I'm talking to you.
You told me,
I'll come down to help you,
I asked,
what about your job,
ones got to do;
What they have to do.
then you came and helped,
to care for me,
for several days,
you showed,
were able to love me,
In many ways.
For what you were willing to do,
you showed me,
you loved me,
Now I can love you too.

Who Am I, I can't Remember

I feel a seizure coming on,
I can't do anything to stop it,
From coming on.
Acting out violently
so somebody would know,
what's happening to me,
Fearing the next day I won't see.
I wake up in the hospital, tired and confused,
my tongue is bitten up,
I have a migraine; feeling I was abused.
I'm looking at all people, that are around me,
not able to recognize any of them,
Oh God; I lost my memory.
After having six seizures,
I can't remember who's who,
after being released, I can't recall;
What I used to do.
We walk into my care provider's game place,
the regular people are there, playing games,
Yet I can't recall; anyone's face.
There's a little girl, who sits down next to me,
I don't recognize her, who is she.
My care provider say's she's your daughter,
and that boy over there, is he your son,
How come I can't remember.
I beg my care provider, please take me to that place,
that's supposable my home,

I don't recognize it; I need to be alone.
Once again having seizures,
Has killed more of my brain cells,
the ones that hold precious memories,
so when will that last one happen?
the one that takes away all my abilities?.

My care provider's income from the gaming place,
wasn't enough to keep it open,
feeling he failed,
Leaving a sad look on his face.

Letting Go Of Your Dreams

You may not have succeeded,
in the gaming business,
but I don't look down on you for it,
I definitely don't love you any less.
You tried to make life easier and happier,
So you could come and go at your leisure.
It's okay if you try something
and fall, that doesn't mean
you should give up,
And say the heck with it all.
If you just believe in yourself more,
you may see, you have the knowledge,
To open another gaming store.
You're not the type,
to just give upon your dreams,
you once told me,
you can make anything happen;
No matter how hard it seems.
Why are these words true for me,
but not you, did you just speak those words,
To lift my spirits?
Are you saying, these words aren't true.
You've attempted to do things,
all your life, but tried again,
How is this different? I ask as your wife.

My other son started stealing,
I had something in a certain place,
I'd ask if anyone seen it,
A guilty looks; was on your face.

My daughter started acting out,
when hearing a different answer,
She would begin; to scream and shout.

Giving Yourself

You say you love me,
yet as soon as I set my purse down,
You steal my money.
I'm out on the patio, cooking our meal,
and you go into my bedroom,
To see what else; you can steal.
Having to put locks, on all the doors,
so that you can't, go into my room,
And steal anymore.
I have struggled all my life,
to get us where we are today,
what gives you the right,
To come and take it away.
You watch your sister,
being punished, for your stupidity,
Yet you say you love her,
that isn't the way, you show love to somebody.
I think it's pretty sad,
everything's under lock and key,
otherwise my child, comes into my room,
And steals it from me.
I hope God, teaches you a lesson,
for your sake,
for it's better to give; than to take
When will those word you say,
be words that are true,
sorry mom,

I won't do that again to you.
My son kept making me seize,
like I told his worker,
and his actions,
are making me seize worst.
I told the worker,
To improve his wealth.
I had to get legal help,
to teach him about his health,
he wouldn't listen to me;
I couldn't teach him myself.
My physician told him,
your mom's dying,
these words he spoke to you,
You thought he was lying.

My Child I'm Doing This For Your Own Good

Son I'm doing for you,
It's not because I don't love you,
because I do,
And want the best for you.
I have to find a place that can teach you,
you won't do what it takes to learn at home,
so what do you expect me to do?
I love you so much inside,
I feel hurt in my heart,
I'm putting you here to learn,
Not to be apart.
I don't want you to live on the streets
From lack of knowledge,
you won't make it, on the streets,
Just get trained; then go to college.
Once again I feel,
I failed as a mom,
you have no goals in life,
neither did your bother;
His future is gone.
Sometimes I feel,
you don't love me,
you show anger towards me,
for being the mom;
I was supposed to be.

knowing you accomplished one thing,
so I could that smiling face,
before God takes me,
To that peaceful place.

It seemed like a chain link,
one putting stress on another,
missing your pills,
because what others may think;
Just like your brother.
You refuse to believe,
your condition made you ill,
you called pastor my Pastor for help,
Stating; yes I will.
Doing The Lords Work
You can to help my son,
after telling you and me,
He didn't want none.
He asked my Pastor,
Please help me, for I was wrong
you were telling the truth;
All along.
I had no money,
to pay for his pills
you then came forth,
to pay for them,
So my son wouldn't get ill.
I stood next to you,

while you paid the lady,
you didn't give up on my brother,
like his friends;
And certain family.

Blue Is Beautiful

Blues represent times in your life,
for time you served your country,
the creation of you children,
and meeting that woman;
Who's still your wife.
The dark blue is when you,
went out serving our country,
asking God, is this what you want;
Me to be.
The baby blue,
is love given to your children,
love created with My Pastor's wife and you,
receiving a love, that's everlasting;
And true.
cobalt is that color in the sky,
My Pastor's wife and you,
still standing next to each other,
For your love; shall never die.
Cover up with it,
when you or My Pastor's wife,
start feeling cold,
the love between you two;
Will never grow old.

CHAPTER 9

⁌⁜⁋

My care provider's parents held holiday dinner,
at their home one certain year,
My care provider heard,
his sister's family was there;
I was happy no fear.
I met the famil of my my brother's girlfriend,
once again, I was able,
to talk to a female;
Comfortably.
I'll never forget,
things mom taught me,
I now had the ability,
To talk to my brother's girlfriend.
I had only a few hours,
to talk to my brother's girlfriend,
but felt close to her;
In just one day.
Time came to leave,
mom and dad's place,
I got the door,
needing to turn back;
To hug my brother's girlfriend once more.

My Friend From God

Your brother introduced us,
several years ago,
I felt I could trust you,
you wouldn't be here today;
Gone tomorrow.
Every time you come back,
to the United States,
I try to spend time with you,
That's what making; a friendship takes.
You have a friendship ring,
from me,
that was my way, of showing myself,
Lifetime friends; are a possibility.
You keep an open mind,
and have a big heart,
thousands of miles from the other,
Feeling like were not apart.
The last time you came,
to your parents place,
the ring on your finger,
A smile came upon my face.
It was getting late,
our family had to leave,
I'd get to the door,
turn around to hug you again;
It was too good to believe.

The following Saturday,
my Pastor asked,
any other announcements,
My Pastor's wife said "we'll be leaving,
For the retreat;" on Thursday,
I asked my daughter,
"Will you go with me?
I'd like you to go,
so we can be together,
You would have time; to be with me."
my daughter nor I,
have been there before,
we could see the wilderness,
We could go outside; and explore.
you get to go outside,
I only see the house walls,
I need you to go, in case I fall.
her friend,
spent all her time with others,
she made new ones
Through her older brother.
The school found pot,
found in my sons locker,
he swore it was his friends,
The friend said; you're a liar.
I wasn't allowed to drive,
because of my disability,
the school said get here,
you'll have to wait;

So My care provider can bring me.
I asked my daughter,
"you still going with me,"
after she said "yes,"
I called My Pastor's wife.
During the sermon,
next Saturday,
they told us what to bring,
When to be ready; on what day.
Time came to leave my care provider,
I hid the poem under his pillow,
I knew he'd find it; then read it too.
my daughter and me were nervous,
what kind of things they did,
Or just a regular service.
I'd look at the trees,
and the mountains,
wondering next year,
if she would be coming;
With me again.
After arriving to the retreat,
My Pastor's daughter told everybody,
take your stuff to your rooms,
Then return; it was time to eat.
My mom told me,
"I can't go this year,"
her husband was dying;
She needed to be here.
He was dying quickly,

my mom knew,
she could go next year when
She promised to go with me.
my daughter said,
"it happens for a reason,"
but the effects,
from continuous seizures;
The end being pleasing.
she told me "that's a good thing,
you and grandma can be together,
And go on stage; and sing."
She made more friends,
talking about things,
they had in common,
Asking why does it have to end.
The schedule at the retreat,
had the thing free time,
she talked,
about certain experiences,
I'd talk about mine.
Everyone was paired,
up with a prayer partner,
at nighttime,
she talked to hers for hours.
There was a certain woman,
I wanted talk to,
but she said I have to go,
Every time I tried to.
my daughter told me,

she's glad she came with me,
she heard testimonies,
other women gave, that made her;
Feel lucky.
My Pastor's daughter gave time
for the ladies to speak,
one lady about feeling strong,
But when she came, she felt weak.
She was an incarcerated prisoner,
learning to just believe and receive,
That God would also love her.
I gave a testimony,
about my mother not loving me,
until I almost died, then My
care provider called her;
She came to me.

I'll cherish this time we had together,
this precious memory of you and I,
I'll remember forever.
It was time to leave the building,
outside, prayer partners and friends,
Saying goodbye while crying.
I told my daughter,
It's okay be back next year,
see friends again,
And the ones we hold dear.
I seen so many,
feelings and emotions in Nicole,

maybe this trip is what she needed,
To have respect me.
While heading home in the city,
viewing the beautiful plants and trees,
knowing soon I'd be home,
With the man; that loved me.
We arrived at home finally,
I seen my care provider standing,
in the house he cleaned,
And had dinner ready for me.
After dinner,
She went down the street,
to see her friend,
hoping when I seen her again,
Her loving side; didn't come to an end.
My son
could care less, about us coming home,
his life was computers;
And that alone.
When that girl of mine,
had came back home,
wasn't the same one, at the retreat
Was she lying?
She started wanting things,
I couldn't afford to get,
we have too many bills,
To fit that into our budget.
My daughter and son,

went to school every day,
while I did my woodwork,
since my ability to be outside;
Was taken away.

A Daughter With A Cold Heart

You have become a cold hearted,
unloving, uncaring, young lady,
what right do you have;
To take my beautiful daughter from me.
You have
so much coldness inside you,
when someone tries to express,
that they love you,
You don't know what to do.
How can you expect,
God to answer your prayers,
if don't believe in him,
That isn't fair.
I really feel for you,
for I'll go to heaven when I die,
How about you.
You must be able to believe,
to see,
that's why my grandma and brother,
Had come to see me.
You only see,
what you want to see,
how can you tell me, how my relationship,
With my mother should be.
I am your Mother, I will always love you,
teaching you right from wrong,
Is what loving parents do?

No matter what you say to me,
or do, you can't take away
My love for you.
My only hope for you,
is that you open that cold heart,
So you experience, the feel of love too.

I find myself talking to my care provider's father,
about my brother not taking his pills,
Getting violent and mean.
You did your best your children,
you can just give advice,
they'll turn you off;
Or hopefully listen.
I took my care provider's father's advice,
and took my son to my doctor,
My doctor told him,
"your killing your mom;
And need to move on."
My body was breaking down internally,
I told my son,
"I'm not going to let you kill me."
I told him,
"I should be wheelchair bound,
Or not even around."

Undying love

You took me to my doctors office,
he said you're dying,
yet today your by my side,
you showed me
when we took our vows;
You weren't lying.

Your parents,
helped me through tragedies,
nobody else to lean on,
For they; didn't want to hear me.
When of none of my family cared,
your family gave time to me,
They knew how to share.

My Four Best Friends #1

Because of my care provider's gracious parents,
who came into my life,
they helped me to accept God,
And is a better wife.
God loves all,
you just have to believe,
offer help somebody,
It's better to give; than receive.
I found my special one in my life,
when I'm with him,
I know one day;
I'll be his wife.
Words can't express,
what these four people mean to me,
the words non-existent
Can it really be.
I pray one day,
God will lead Alex to my care provider,
so our family will be whole,
My care provider can say; son I love you.
I've been given.
the most understanding mother,
she's done things, not expected of her;
And wouldn't wish for another.
She's been there, like a mother would be,
if all mom's were like her,
A perfect world; it would be.

Dad taught me,
that because I make mistakes,
doesn't mean,
I'm not deserving of his love,
Correcting it is all it takes.
I'm closer to God,
than I have been in my life,
thanks to my care provider's words,
I'll see God; till then be care provider's wife.
with the first creating the last three,
turning out so right,
It must have meant to be.

My care provider said, "it's okay honey,
in a couple months,
the problems will be gone,"
For three days.
My mother called,
telling me her husband died,
I couldn't help her, except comfort her;
While she cried.
His mother,
was told about it, she refused
To believe it, and didn't want to hear it.
My mother was to do everything,
she told my step dad's mom, "your son is dead,"
Yelling to mom; get out your lying.
After that day,
she never left her home,

just lie in bed all day,
She just wanted to be alone.
It was hard for mom,
to constantly care for her,
the distance between their homes,
Made it harder.
My mom called every day,
crying and wishing,
It would just go away.
I'd try to comfort mom,
speak about the retreat,
then for three day's
It will be gone.
Stress from her pain,
made my body seize,
looking up and stating
It's make believe.
First my mom loses her son,
the same year hasn't passed,
And now loses her husband.
Trying to be there for mom,
and watch over my son,
if I took my eyes off him,
Something was gone.
My son's life was his computer,
my brother died,
the same year, mom's husband died;
He had no remorse for he.
I hoped he would quit

doing stupid things in school,
I wanted him to graduate,
Stop being a fool.
It was almost time to leave,
so I had to hide everything,
though he said don't worry,
It wasn't words; one could believe.
Every time the phone would ring,
I feared the words, I can't go
To the retreat, deal with anything.
My mom lost my brother, and her husband
to cancer, the same year,
In 2006 she lost two people,
She held dear.
Mom moved into my care provider's home,
to help him care for me,
so when my care provider went to work,
I wouldn't be alone.
After the hurricane had happened,
My mom donated her trailer,
So she could help them.
It helped me by mom living here,
My care provider now had peace of mind,
instead of wondering,
Or having a feeling; of fear.
My mom and I spoke frequently,
about the ladies retreat,
Being able to relax, and kick up her feet.
Nurses no longer, coming to her home,

telling her, it won't be long,
fearing the remainder of her life;
She'd be alone.
My mom and I spent daily time together,
Why wasn't I invited,
to spend time with you mother,
yet your husband would offer time;
To my brothers.
Why didn't you stop my cousin,
making me do nasty things,
She didn't know, he
Was; or to siblings.
Kid's think parent's to know everything,
anger built inside me for years,
Because nobody did anything.
For having this discussion,
between my mom and me,
Released allot of hostility.
Were suddenly interrupted,
someone was calling,
my stepdad said he needed help,
He had just fallen.
he had asked for my mom,
he told her he needed help,
she packed certain things,
Asking her; what's wrong.
Mom went to his place every day,
came home in the evening,
He was quickly slipping away.

he wanted to see me,
saying that's fine,
gave his address to me,
It blew my mind.
When getting to his place,
asking me to talk to him alone,
Looking at him face to face.
I reported this man, for molesting me,
Why would he want to see me?
While he and I, looked at each
other, he said, "I'm so sorry;
I lied to your mother.
What I did for you was wrong,
I don't want to go to hell,
how do I get God, to forgive me;
I'm not well."
I called Pastor my Pastor one night,
Larry's dying,
wants his relationship with God,
To be right.
Larry repeated words,
that my Pastor,
told me to say,
So Larry could be saved.
Repent of your sins,
he did that my Pastor,
After I' came to see him.
Larry stated he believes,
Jesus is the son of God,

Jesus to come into my heart;
Then give yourself to God. Mom
went to Larry's,
his body weaker every day,
to find our maker,
Had taken him away.
After my care provider's father and
my care provider is teaching me,
about heaven with hate,
I learned to forgive,
So I could one day; enter that Gate.
Because of past situations,
like this, guilt and hatred,
Was lifted; I got my wish.
Killers or rapists in prison,
sometimes repeat things,
thinking they'll never see heaven;
And meet the king.
Larry thought the same thing,
till he and I talked,
it's then he learned,
just do what's right;
You can see our king.

Am I Crazy

This man calls me,
letting me know he's dying,
I'm asking you to forgive me,
for what I did to you;
And starts crying.
Over thirty years ago,
Larry was my stepdad,
raped me nine years later,
Taking all I had.
He never admitted what he'd done,
he swore he never did it,
leaving me to feel,
I was the guilty one.
Twenty-four years later,
he said forgive me,
I already have, to our maker;
You must plea.
Larry's dying,
from what's called cancer,
turning to God now,
Is the only answer.

I tried comforting my mom,
I told her,
Larry gave himself to God,
before his
Life on earth; was gone.

Mom kept her word to my care provider,
will she go to the retreat,
With me, keeping her promise to me too.
We talked about good times,
we had in our life,
I spoke about being blessed,
With care provider; forever being his wife.
Sadly my mom couldn't say,
the same thing,
for her partners passed way,
Having nobody; or nothing.
I told mom what the retreat was like,
for my daughter and me,
Saying you'll have fun; wait and see.
I was explained of certain
events there,
watching her face,
to see if excitement was there;
Or did she care.
I apologized for outrages,
expressed towards her,
telling her, I want a relationship;
One that was better.
I don't hold the past against her,
yet it upsets her,
when I read a poem about it,
Using it; to reach another.
There's reasons,
for the bad in our lives,

sometimes taking years,
finding out why;
Then learn how it applies.
I asked my mom,
to go to church with me,
instructions are being given tonight,
By My Pastor's wife.
She will tell us what to bring,
The cost of it, and who would be driving.
After services was over,
she socialized with others,
Didn't walk out the church and run.
It took me years to understand,
why one's life is easier,
another is on the corner,
Holding out their hand.
Mom you are special to me,
you tried making me strong,
When others would laugh at me.

For Her Words Were True

I can't believe,
I got my mom to come with me,
staring at her to see it's real,
For I felt this moment, could never be.
After leaving here last year,
I almost died from seizures,
not being able to say I love you,
To her; was my biggest fear.
Before this medical tragedy,
I didn't realize, what I meant to her,
Or her to me.
We never were really close,
to each other,
not because love wasn't there,
Our separation; caused by another.
Three days before coming here,
when the phone rang,
asking is it her,
Will she say; those words I fear.
I want you to know,
I'm proud of you,
you kept your promise,
And did; what you said you would do.
For this is the first time,
we have done anything together,
But the memory will last forever.
Thank you for being able,

to show love to me,
coming to the retreat,
Made beautiful and lasting memories; with me.
I felt you didn't love me,
by coming to the retreat,
I seen a side of you;
I wasn't able to see.
It's now time for us to go,

first I wrote my poem to my care provider,
Then slip it underneath his pillow.
The ladies met at the church,
in the parking lot,
mom liked not having to drive,
It gave her time to look allot.
After we would reach Denver,
we stop to stretch or eat,
I knew inside myself,
We would soon be there.
My care provider had put funds away,
so mom and I could go places,
On free time day.
Mom met lot's of ladies there,
seen how they were,
Having love in their hearts; and care.
They handed us a bag,
everything inside of it,
We would need even name tags.
My Pastor's daughter would show us,

where we would be sleeping,
I just felt like it wasn't real,
Like a dream.
It was hard to sleep at night,
Mom and I talked,
both of us learning about the other,
It couldn't have been more right.
I seen that loving side of her,
being able to bond together,
wouldn't have been possible,
If I had to come without her.
I love my mom more now,
than I ever did in the past,
from lack of communication,
Made me feel like an outcast.
Certain family members,
get embarrassed about my book,
they think,
I'm cutting them down; that's their outlook.
You cared for us kids and our father,
he abused you, for not doing things,
The way he liked; why bother.
Larry only worked,
if you went with him and worked too,
Now look what it's physically, done to you.
For this is our last day here,
I never want to lose your love,
I say this from my heart; totally sincere.
You went outside to walk with me,

seeing wildlife here,
When I'm home; I'd never see.
The Good That Comes From Bad #2
There was a time, I felt you didn't love me
Hard times, is all life seemed to be.
Even when we were apart, you were inside me.
Grounded, for doing bad things
Outside our home, I learned what honesty brings.
Our lives, may not have been the best
Daily learning, I didn't have to be; like the rest.
Through all the bad, that occurred in my life,
Heartbroken until a man made me his wife.
Although my life, may not have been easy,
That's what made me, who God wanted me to be.
Constantly conquering trials, in your life,
Overcoming the addictions made you a better wife.
Making the decision, yes or no every day,
Eventually God gave you strength to turn it away,
So that's what made you, who you are today.
For years you and I never did anything together
Realizing that God may take me forever
Overwhelmed with feelings of regret
Made you come forth, a day I'll never forget.
By us becoming who we are today,
Allowed us, to love one another,
Doing what God wanted us to do
took the emptiness away.
Hoping my son,
would quit his acts of stupidity,

See and accept abilities, taken from me.
I learned I was dying,
but I refused to give up,
And quit trying.
What was supposed to happen,
several years ago,
is beginning now,
I feel the pain from it;
I should know.
My care provider helped me learn,
what I needed to know,
therefore, when I pass;
I know where I'll go.
My son's actions,
kept causing extreme stress,
his pants showing half his rear,
His bedroom was always a mess.
I told my care provider, "I can't
take anymore of this,
wanting to seize over and over,"
To get away from this.
I was having many of them,
I didn't think,
I'd see my care provider's face again.
Times when my son stressed me out,
I would go to my bedroom,
And write what that day was about.

I Will Watch Over You

I finally found a love who could be true
Well God is calling me home now
I will still be able to see you
Look up to the stars at night,
Let god show you, I'm all right.
Although I'm not here physically,
Let your heart know I'll never
forget what you've done for
me.
When all there was, was hatred in my heart
All it took from you, was patience and kindness.
You showed me, a man could love
me, yet not tear my world
apart.
Slowly but surely, I opened the doors to my heart.
Letting you show me, you were different,
One with patience and love, to guide me from sin.
Vows we made to each other before Christ,
Enables me, to want to be here with you
You showed me to love another can be nice.
Once again I say I will always love you
Understand that one-day, you'll be here too.

CHAPTER 10

~∞~

My care provider went to work on Saturday,
lunch time he called me,
he told me I no longer,
Had to be a payee.
I prayed to God nightly,
asking God to guide him,
to succeed in something,
Then maybe, create a family.
The heart in my son, is very cold,
I can no longer teach him,
The inside of me; is weak and old.
Kids expect parents to do everything,
I tried to teach him, to pay bills,
I can only do my budgeting.
He didn't want to hear it,
he just figured,
Someone else would do it.
Not having goals,
that he could possibly succeed,
not getting back up,
Telling himself; I will proceed.
I was proud he graduated,
for completing school,
I kept constantly crying,
Feeling like a fool.
I couldn't convince him,
to work towards a success,
after graduating, his life;
Was a mess?

I went to bed crying every night,
no word from my daughter in months,
Wondering if she was all right.
Asking myself,
Now what did I not do right.
I kept visualizing my daughter,
speaking about her succeeding,
Because of love from my mother.
I congratulated my son, and asked,
what he was interested in doing,
saying;
I don't know how to do nothing.
he constantly said,
he didn't want to talk about it now,
since nobody will help me,
I can't learn how.
My care provider and my mom asked him too,
get outraged,
while walking out the door, saying
I don't know what to do.
Mom told me,
I just asked a question,
saying one day,
He will learn; a hard lesson.
My oldest had dropped out,
my daughter left home,
thinking she knew,
What life was about.
Yelling at my care provider,

for things he never knew,
But for what my kids, would say; or do.
My care provider was the kind of man,
people search for their lifetime,
Knowing inside, he was meant; to be mine.
I feel I have the best mate,
for he gives love,
Even when my actions, show hate.

I Will Always Love You

You're not only my lover,
but also my friend,
we held together,
From beginning to end.
All things happen, for a reason,
when I look at you,
All I see; is pleasing.
God don't hand out,
what you can't do,
we wouldn't be together,
my dream;
Wouldn't have came true.
We've been together for years,
dealing with good and bad,
I'm no longer alone, for that I'm glad.
Your more a man,
than words can say,
nothing in this world,
Can take that away.
I know you're my soul mate,
I can only,
feel overwhelming love for you,
You I could never hate.
You have filled the inside of me,
where no more is empty,
You embracing me, is more than plenty.
When I'm down,

from not having allot,
re-assuring me it's okay,
We'll make it, with what we got.
I find it impossible, to stay mad at you,
I look into your beautiful eyes,
Violent feeling is gone; because of you.

I was depressed for almost a year,
Nicole called about her graduation,
All I could do was shed tears.
Nicole hardly visited,
waiting till graduation day,
like she barely knew me,
Taking that motherly feeling away.
Seeing her,
less than ninety minutes,
Feeling like someone tore out my guts.
Mom was telling me "it's okay,
just a couple more months,
We'll go to the retreat, and get away."
Now mom was comforting me,
because of losing a loved one,
my other kid's attitude was,
I don't care; I'm done.
Praying to God at night,
asking that he take me home,
one I thought loved me,
take away this pain; from being alone.
If I woke up the next day,

I knew there was a reason,
He wasn't ready; to take me away.
I had to still keep my house up,
telling my kid, the senators office,
Was still helping me; I'm not giving up.
The senators right hand man,
heard what he was doing to me,
And said; "I'll do what I can."
I was mentally fading,
from my condition, He wouldn't get a payee,
Placing me; in a bad position.
He went to see his worker,
telling her I was kicking him out,
he didn't bother telling her,
I had to have; a caretaker.
Once again,
a loved one tells me I'm here,
when expressing my feelings;
They run in fear.
My siblings block me from their lives,
because of being different,
They won't introduce me, to their wives.
God gave me five brothers,
God took one away,
Only two of them listen to what I say.
My brain,
slowly peeling my memory away,
I don't know words like before,
My kids can't believe it; then walk away.

I told my mom,
"he has to get out on his own,"
he gave up his benefits,
Now he doesn't even have a home.
Every time I hear the song,
don't laugh at me, I remember kids
Laughing at me in school, when I seized.
When my son was in elementary,
he sometimes would seize,
then ask me not to make him go back,
They all tease and laugh at me.
From that time on,
His self-esteem went downhill,
watching him seize while asleep,
Because he no longer takes his pills.
People outside our house,
cutting him down, while laughing at him,
He refused to get up; and try again.
Calling the senator on a weekly basis,
explaining,
I can't remember my own pills,
how can the government expect me;
To remember his.
In our house,
were only words of complaining,
only hearing words of love,
When my care provider and I, were alone speaking.
Tensions caused me to go the hospital,
seeing high numbers, from my implant,

My doctor asked; "is it your son."
Then why do I see my dead brother,
I had a strong love for,
My doctor's conclusion was,
Must be an aura.
Time was near for the ladies retreat,
if I see him again, will his hand and mine;
Be able to meet.
Shall My son come while I'm there,
will it be then God tells me,
you tried reaching out,
They didn't care.
I wrote my yearly poem to my care provider,
expressing my love for him,
Like I did, when we said; I do.
I wrote this to my brother My son,
he was convinced, I'd forget him,
I listen to two songs monthly;
Remembering him.
I hurt seeing him in pain,
while slowly dying,
my Pastor heard his cry,
My brother is where; angels fly.

We Shall Meet Again

Your only gone a little while,
when our time comes,
Again we will see your smile.
You may not be physically here,
I still whisper secrets to you,
Knowing you able to hear.
We will come to you,
when it's our time,
keeping memories of you,
In our heart; and minds.

I told my care provider, "If I don't return,
it's because God came,
To take me home," a lesson to be learned.
My Pastor's wife spoke about the retreat
on Saturday,
telling us to bring,
Only what was necessary.
Mom told My Pastor's wife, "we
didn't have a vehicle,"
she agreed to pick us up,
Inside it wcre several people.
My Pastor's daughter does the
arranging and scheduling,
members of her church,
do the cooking and cleaning,
We didn't have to do anything.

She always made sure,
her sister and mom,
My mom and I, were put together.
Since we were packed,
and ready to go,
I wrote my care provider his poem,
Then put it under his pillow.
I felt guilty the first year,
like I left a part of me behind,
Going to bed crying tears.
The church van arrived at my place,
seeing I was physically able to go,
Put a smile on several faces.
Seeing friends,
that only went on Sundays,
seeing them going again,
Put a smile on my face.
My Pastor's wife packed our stuff,
so it was accessible,
so I could get to it,
When it was time for pills.
Thanks to the church in peyton,
and by the grace of God,
I survived another year,
To re-unite with women; I hold dear.
God gave me another year,
to spend time with my mom,
don't take time for granted,
For anytime; it can be gone.

It's my fourth year,
we have came here together,
Mom I'll remember you forever.
My care provider had me call him in Denver,
giving him peace of mind,
Knowing we were almost there.
Some women fell asleep,
I tried to sleep also,
my medicines,
Wouldn't allow me to do so.
when arriving at the retreat,
Dinner had been cooked, and ready to eat.
God allowed me to come another year,
to spend time with my mom,
showing love towards her,
Before my time is gone.
I love spending time with My Pastor's daughter,
she makes it possible,
To meet new people, and see my friends.
This is the fourth time,
mom has came with me,
time to do thing together,
How precious can it be.
We stayed at the cabin,
instead of going to town,
taking time to talk,
And walk around.
Talking to people from last year,
I got really close to Carie,

I didn't want to think,
About leaving here.
Mom and I,
learn about each other every year,
she help care for me,
Everyday I'm here.
My Pastor's daughter brings her cross every year,
I ask God to give doctors knowledge,
So next year I can be here.
The purpose of the cross,
My Pastor's daughter brings,
so you can give troubles to God,
Stuff I cannot do, impossible things.
I should be wheelchair bound,
by the grace of God,
I still have the ability, to walk around.
God gave strength to my daughter Nicole,
so I wouldn't be nervous,
about coming the first time for me,
My care provider taught me,
how to let go,
of the hatred and stubbornness,
I had a heart of emptiness.
I told My Pastor's daughter since last year,
now two of sibling loved me,
and two could care less,
Maybe they'll open their eyes; and see.

I thank mom for coming with me,
If God takes me,
before two thousand eleven;
Know that I'm in heaven.

My Everlasting Gift

The Lord enabled my body,
To come here with my mom.
doing things, and spending time together,
Will make us more strong.
Doctors saying,
I wouldn't be coming along,
I won't be able to come here with mom,
Having no ability; to form a bond.
I look at the beautiful mountains,
God took time to create,
I'm standing next to a woman,
I used to hate.
I ask God,
to take my problems away,
For I cannot live like this, day after day.
Other females had their mom,
not being able to see her for years,
I asked my care provider; why
won't she let me see her.
I had a seizure,
at my care provider's gaming place
he laid me on the floor,
I ask please God, let me see her once more.
When I woke up, My mother was standing there,
I said you supposed to be at work,
you'll lose your job,
Mom said right now I don't care.

Ever since this tragedy had happened to me,
my mom and I, spend quality time together,
See god heard me.
Thank you mom, for spending
another year with me,
I love you so much, for time you've given me.
My care provider asked if you would move in,
so you would be with me daily,
then he didn't have,
to call every half hour;
It helped mentally.
I love you now and forever,
nobody can take our special bond away,
For we learned how to love each other.

It's like mom committed her time to me,
taking me to the doctors,
Staying during the days with me.
Nicole called saying" what to I do,
having no place to live,
And I'm seven months pregnant too."
I couldn't tell her you know better,
when I did the same thing,
I was younger than her.
I told Nicole to come home,
with her boyfriend,
but My son in law had to get a job,
Or it would come to an end.
Nicole arrived at my door,

after opening it,
I didn't recognize her anymore.
Nicole was seven months in pregnancy,
it reminded me,
When I carried my oldest in me.
After giving birth to my first baby,
they brought in,
A nine pound ten-ounce baby to me.
Nicole is a little smaller luckily,
she still has two months,
Before delivery.
Nicole's scared she won't have,
what the baby needs,
I said "you'll make it,
As long as My son in law provides.
You're still that girl God gave me,
the love I feel for you,
nobody can change that in me,
In me."
My son in law just needs to get a job,
so he can care for you and the baby,
And not lay around like a slob.
Years ago I cried like a baby,
because you left for college,
Then my daughter; became a lady.
I don't look down on you,
for the four years of going to college,
Trying to figure out, what you wanted to do.
I felt a heavy weight lifted from me,

then we couldn't be in the same room,
You no longer respected me.
After talking two days face to face,
learning about each other again,
Not having to make you, find another place.
I lost allot of years with her,
now were able to get along,
Share the love and laughter.
I love you for understanding how I feel,
I want you to know,
That my love for you will always be real.

She Believed In Me

This girl walked into my door,
the thirty first of many,
we just hugged each other,
Having lots; to say.
Her vocabulary wasn't like mine,
her words weren't pleasing,
The girl that left here; was left behind.
I asked Nicole to not speak,
that word in my house anymore,
If you can't respect me, walk out the door.
Efforts were made by talking to each other,
now we can get along,
By one listening to another.
My first pregnancy was scary,
I just wanted it to be healthy,
Not have a disability; like me.
I gave birth to two boys and a girl,
trying to teach Nicole,
What was waiting, in that big world.
I had my little girl in October,
no matter what you feel about me,
My love for you will never be over.
Hoping your feelings of love,
continue for My son in law through eternity,
Being your soul mate, like my care provider and me.
I'll do what I can for you,
you also need to understand,

I don't have the knowledge I used to.
Shall I offend you or My son in law,
because of something I say,
ask me what I mean,
Instead of walking away.
When you and My son in law create your family,
don't exclude me from your life,
Because of my loss of vocabulary.
I hope you can still love me,
as I lose certain abilities,
For you'll always be my baby girl for eternity.